Ezra Pound's *Cathay*

Wai-lim Yip

Ezra
Pound's
Cathay

PRINCETON UNIVERSITY PRESS

PRINCETON, NEW JERSEY 1969

Publication of this book has been
aided by the Whitney Darrow Publication Reserve Fund
of Princeton University Press.

This book has been composed in Granjon type.

Printed in the United States of America
by Princeton University Press

for Ezra Pound
if he wants it

preface

TEN YEARS ago, when I translated T. S. Eliot's *Waste Land* into Chinese,[1] and two years later, when I wrote a thesis on his poetry, I wondered what sort of poem *The Waste Land* was before Ezra Pound laid hands on it. I had hoped that someone close to Eliot could examine his original manuscript and make public the process of transformation so that we could tell for sure in what way the poem could be rightly called Eliot's and how much of it was actually Pound's own work. A comparison of the original *Waste Land* and its present form would be useful as a revelation of Pound's mind at work. We would be able to understand the peculiar methods by which he incorporated his own principles into Eliot's.

The present attempt to examine the poems in *Cathay* as translations—focusing upon the three stages: the original, Fenollosa's English crib, and Pound's version—is aimed at a similar understanding of the poet's mind at work. The major difficulty in this kind of study is the unavailability of the manuscript. Due to some legal complications, which I need not go into here, access to the Fenollosa notebooks is denied for an uncertain period of time.

However before the notebooks were sealed, three scholars had read, recorded, and published several examples. These are: the text of "Song of the Bowmen of Shu" and a poem by Oshorei [i.e. Wang Ch'ang-ling][2] in Lawrence W. Chisolm's *Fenollosa: The Far East and American Culture* (1963); the annotations for "The Beautiful Toilet" in *Ezra Pound: Perspectives*, edited by Noel Stock (1965); and several examples

---

[1] Published in *Ch'uang-shih-chi* (*The Epoch Poetry Quarterly*), No. 16 (Kaohsiung, Taiwan, January 1961), 28-39.

[2] Although Pound did not translate this one, it is still worthwhile to include it in the Appendix because it shows the format of Fenollosa's transcription.

in Hugh Kenner's "The Invention of China" (1967).[3] I am indebted to these fragments for the present study. Mrs. Dorothy Pound has been most generous in extending her assistance. She kindly allowed me to use a copy of Fenollosa's glosses on the "Lament of the Frontier Guard" that Mr. Kenner possessed. I am particularly grateful to the latter who not only sent me that copy but also allowed me to have a carbon copy of "The Invention of China" several months before he published it in *Spectrum*. He also answered freely some of my questions concerning misprints and revisions in *Cathay*.

All the above cribs are reprinted with proper acknowledgments for their sources in Appendix I. One poem, the text of "The Unmoving Cloud," which is in the University of Virginia Library, is not reprinted. I believe Mr. Kenner's treatment of it in his article covers all the pertinent points.

In order that the reader can have an idea of the general format of the Chinese poems and the original line units, I have provided in Appendix II literal translations of all the *Cathay* poems, facing Pound's versions. I have also numbered the lines for the sake of comparison.

I also wish to express my gratitude to Professors Robert Fagles and A. W. Litz, both of Princeton University, for turning me back from other distractions toward this present study. The latter, in supervising the writing of my original dissertation, has been most sympathetic and helpful. He recommended many significant improvements in style and organization. Thanks are due to Professor Kao Yu-kung, also of Princeton University, for taking the trouble of going over my translations and correcting some of the errors therein, and to Professor F. Mote, Chairman of the Oriental Studies Department, Princeton University, for his warm and helpful

---

[3] *Spectrum*, IX.1 (Spring 1967), 30-31. (See Appendix I.) Kenner also includes in this article the annotations for "The Beautiful Toilet."

criticism of parts of the book. To Professor Edmund Keeley I owe several hours of discussion on the problem of presentation in the second and the third chapters. Professor Roy Harvey Pearce of the University of California at San Diego has assisted me in various ways for which I would like to acknowledge my gratitude. My wife's encouragement and love are beyond acknowledgment here.

WAI-LIM YIP

University of California at San Diego
1967

acknowledgments

I WANT to express my deep appreciation to New Directions for allowing me to use all of Pound's *Cathay* as well as excerpts from *Personae* and *The Cantos*. I also wish to thank Dorothy Pound, Committee for Ezra Pound, for giving me permission to use the Poem "Lament of the Frontier Guard" from the Fenollosa manuscript.

The following authors and publishers graciously gave me permission to quote from books which they have published: Harvard University Press for permission to use some of the verse of Emily Dickinson; Francis A. Johns, Rutgers University Library; Yale University Press; Jonathan Cape, Limited; Paragon Book Reprint Corporation; the Meredith Press of D. Appleton and Company; Harcourt, Brace, and World for permission to quote some of the verse of T. S. Eliot; Alfred Knopf; Houghton Mifflin; Macmillan; A. C. Graham for permission to use verse from *An Anthology of Chinese Literature*, edited by C. Birch and D. Keene, School of Oriental and African Studies, University of London; *Poetry Australia*; Bernhard Karlgren, The Museum of Far Eastern Antiquities, Stockholm; and Hugh Kenner for permission to use his journal articles.

contents

Ezra Pound's *Cathay*

introduction

"Cathay, Translations by Ezra Pound, for the Most
Part from the Chinese of Rihahu, from the Notes
of the Late Ernest Fenollosa, and the Decipherings
of the Professors Mori and Ariga."

With these words, Pound introduced his book of translations
of Chinese poetry in 1915. The books was immediately received with excitement by his contemporaries. Mr. Ford Madox
Hueffer, for example, said, "The poems in *Cathay* are things
of a supreme beauty. What poetry should be, that they are."[1]
But the most formidable statement which has gone solidly
into the opinions of later Pound critics was made by T. S.
Eliot. He called Pound "the inventor of Chinese poetry" and
said that "through his translation we really at last get the
original."[2] There is no indication anywhere that Eliot had
the knowledge of the Chinese language and Chinese poetry to
warrant this influential statement. Mere acquaintance with
Legge and Giles could not qualify him to assume this authority. And yet, for many decades, critics have taken his words
rather seriously. They probably do so not because Eliot is a
qualified judge of Chinese, but because he is a supreme judge
of poetry. And because *Cathay* is at root a group of superb
poems, Pound's total ignorance of the Chinese language does
not seem to have bothered his English readers. In fact, it did
not even bother some Chinese readers. Hsieh Wen-tung, for
instance, has ignored the obvious mistakes Pound has made

[1] Quoted in T. S. Eliot's "Ezra Pound: His Metric and Poetry"
(1917) in *To Criticize the Critic* (London, 1965), p. 181.
[2] Introduction to *Ezra Pound: Selected Poems*, ed., T. S. Eliot (London, 1928), p. 14.

3

and said that Pound's poetic acumen has made up for the loss incurred by linguistic errors.[3] Roy Earl Teele (a sinologist), in his study of English translations of Chinese poetry, *Through a Glass Darkly* (Ann Arbor, 1949), attacks the Fenollosa-Pound approach, but thinks Pound superior to other translators, because these poems are (he borrows Eliot's word here) "translucencies."[4]

To take *Cathay* for a group of excellent English poems based upon some Chinese text rather than for translations as such has become *the* attitude of most Pound critics. Hence Hugh Kenner, the most vigorous interpreter of Pound's poetry, is tempted to sidestep the issue of translation and reads *Cathay* mainly as if they were English poems: "*Cathay* is notable, considered as an English product rather than [as a] Chinese product."[5] He thinks these poems serve "to extend, inform, and articulate the preoccupations of the present by bringing the past abreast of it."[6] "The preoccupations of the present," we are told recently, are those with World War I: "For *Cathay* . . . is largely a war-book, using Fenollosa's much as Pope used Horace or Johnson Juvenal, to supply a system of parallels and a structure of discourse . . . the *Cathay* poems paraphrase, as it were, an elegiac war-poetry nobody wrote. Perfectly vital after half a century, they are among the most durable of all poetic responses to World War I."[7] Although Kenner hints here and there that, as translations, they are equally superb, he never says that they are *positively* so.

What about the merits or demerits of these poems as translations? The reader naturally expects the Chinese scholars to answer this question. But, to our despair, there is scarcely any

[3] "English Translations of Chinese Poetry," *Criterion*, xvii (April 1938), 423.
[4] Pp. 6, 8, 107.
[5] *The Poetry of Ezra Pound* (London, 1951), p. 154.
[6] *Ibid.*, p. 144.
[7] Kenner, "The Invention of China," *Spectrum*, ix.1 (Spring 1967), 30-31. (Hereafter abbreviated as *Spectrum*.)

intelligent discussion at all. Arthur Waley, a regular diner in the Pound group,[8] apparently did not approve these translations, but he did not criticize Pound openly. Soon after the appearance of *Cathay*, he retranslated several of Li Po's poems in *Cathay* in a paper delivered before the China Society at the School of Oriental Studies, London.[9] But his translations there prove no better than Pound's. In fact, his language is very much indebted to Pound's *Cathay*, as we shall see in Chapter III.[10]

Many Chinese scholars simply cannot believe that translations can be made without any knowledge of the language to be translated.[11] Hence, both George Kennedy's essay on Pound's ignorance of the Chinese language[12] and Achilles Fang's article, "Fenollosa and Pound,"[13] in which he catalogues without commentary numerous linguistic errors, deepen the impression that *Cathay* can in no way stand up as translations.

Although the recent joint effort of Pen-ti Lee and Donald Murray claims to do more than Fang,[14] the essay, typical of its kind, ends up in detecting linguistic errors only and fails to probe into the internal thought progress of either the orig-

[8] Iris Barry, "The Ezra Pound Period" in *The Bookman* (October 1931), 167.

[9] *The Poet Li Po, A.D. 701-762* (1918). See also Achilles Fang, "Fenollosa and Pound," *Harvard Journal of Asian Studies*, xx (June 1957), 221.

[10] It is probably for this reason that Waley never reprinted these translations (except one) in his life time.

[11] If Robert Lowell had included some translations from the Chinese in his recent *Imitations* (New York, 1961), a book of excellent translations from many languages he did not know, he would have been under the same attack.

[12] "Fenollosa, Pound and the Chinese Character," *Yale Literary Magazine* cxxvi (December 1958), 24-36.

[13] See note 9.

[14] "The Quality of *Cathay*: Ezra Pound's Early Translations of Chinese Poems," *Literature East and West* x.3 (September 1966), 264-277. (Hereafter abbreviated as *LE&W*.) For concrete example of their criticism, see Chapter III.

inal or the translations.[15] In fact, because they have ignored the Fenollosa manuscript made available by Chisolm and Stock[16] and Pound's own poetry and criticism, their conclusions are often false and lacking in perspective.

The criticisms of *Cathay* (none of which is book-length) fall into two obvious patterns: defense and condemnation. But mere defense or condemnation is bound to blur the true image of these poems. Most of Pound's defenders could not discuss the way in which some of the poems are said to be close to the original in the "sequence of images," "rhythm," "effects," and "tone."[17] Those who condemn Pound tend to concentrate on the scar and overlook everything else.

What is more important at this stage is neither to defend nor to condemn but to understand Pound as fully as we can without being led astray by predetermined conclusions.[18] To achieve such understanding is to widen the possibility of

[15] In the same issue we find two other articles on Pound's early translations, Angela Jung Palandri's "'The Stone is Alive in My Hand'—Ezra Pound's Chinese Translations" and Richard P. Benton's "A Gloss on Pound's 'Four Poems of Departure.'" The former, like her Ph.D. dissertation *Ezra Pound and China*, attends to Pound's general debt to China as seen in the *Cantos* and tries to see the poems in *Cathay* as illustrations of the imagistic theories. (For a summary of her dissertation, see the *Pound Newsletter: 9*, January 1956, pp. 9-10.) Like Lee and Murray, she did not consult the Fenollosa manuscript. The latter, again without resorting to the crib, is concerned with linguistic errors rather than literary tenets.

[16] Lawrence W. Chisolm's *Fenollosa: The Far East and American Culture* (New Haven-London, 1963) gives us the notes for "Song of the Bowmen of Shu," p. 249 and a poem by Oshorei (Wang Ch'angling) which Pound did not translate. See illustrations following page 224. Noel Stock, ed., *Ezra Pound: Perspectives* (Chicago, 1965), gives us the notes for "The Beautiful Toilet" pp. 178-89.

[17] These are Hugh Kenner's searching words (*Translations*, p. 12). Even Kenner's recent article, "The Invention of China," in which he examines several of Fenollosa's cribs, fails to bring out *the* Chinese poems and their bearing upon the translations.

[18] "There were four things from which the Master was entirely free. He had no foregone conclusions, no arbitrary predeterminations, no obstinacy, and no egoism." *Confucian Analects*, Book IX in *The Chinese Classics*, tr., James Legge (Hong Kong, 1871), I, 217.

6

communication, and a clear measurement of Pound's achievement in this case will involve at least the following steps:

1. To look at the problems of translation from Chinese into English, and in particular, to discuss the difficulty of approximating in English the peculiar mode of representation constituted by Chinese syntax.

2. To look into Pound's mind as a poet, to know the obsessive concepts and techniques he cherished *at the time* he translated these Chinese poems and to see how these conditioned his translations.

3. Since Fenollosa annotated these poems under Japanese instructors ("Rihaku," for instance, is the Japanese name for Li Po), it is necessary for us to examine the triple relation, from the original Chinese to Fenollosa's notes and to the end products, in order to find out how the intermediary has obstructed Pound and how his creative spirit sometimes breaks through the crippled text to resurrect what was in the original.

4. No translator can claim to have actually translated the poetry. This is also true of Pound. How close, then, are the "equivalents"[19] he gets out of the Fenollosa notes to the original, the "cuts and turns"[20] of the Chinese poems? In other words, we need to compare carefully the original and the derivative "forms of consciousness" to see what has actually happened in between.

The present study of *Cathay* seeks, therefore, not to defend nor to condemn but to understand Pound by following these steps. It aims at widening the scope of understanding of Pound as poet by discussing his role as translator of Chinese. Hopefully, this will clarify certain stylistic directions in the entire development of Pound's poetry. As we shall see in the following chapters, *Cathay* in many ways forms a pivotal point in his development, and without understanding this no Pound study can claim to be complete.

[19] This is Pound's own term. See Chapter IV.
[20] For concrete examples of these points, see Chapter IV.

chapter one

The Chinese Poem: Some Aspects of the
Problem of Syntax in Translation

In his "Some Reflections on the Difficulty of Translations,"
Achilles Fang has conveniently summed up the three sides
of the problem of translation: (1) "adequate comprehension
of the translated text," (2) "adequate manipulation of the
language translated into," and (3) "what happens in between."[1] As I understand it, the first may be represented by
the scholar-reader, the second by the versifier, and the third
by the poet, with the ghost of a critic behind all three. The
readers must not be deluded by the word "adequate" into
thinking that it means the same as I. A. Richards' "adequate
reader" in which the implied theory of an ideal reader has
led to Eliot's severe criticism in his "Poetry and Propaganda":
"There is, according to my view, not *one*, but a *series*, of ap-
preciators of poetry. One of the errors, I think, of critical
theory, is to conceive one hypothetical poet on the one hand,
and one hypothetical reader on the other."[2] When I borrow
Mr. Fang's neat scheme for the discussion of the problems in
translation, I do not imply (nor does Mr. Fang) *one* hypothetical reading of the text on the one hand and *one* hypo-

---

[1] *On Translation*, ed., Reuben A. Brower (Cambridge, Mass., 1959),
p. 111. Although Mr. Fang's essay deals only with the first aspect,
focusing on the transmission of the prose meaning rather than the
poetic meaning, this summary is a neat scheme for the present discussion.

[2] *Bookman*, 70 (February 1930), 595-602, reprinted in *Literary
Opinion in America* ed., Zabel (New York, 1951), p. 103.

thetical interpretation on the other. Different persons, dictated to by their specific education and preoccupations, always tend to see different things in the same material. Total comprehension, implying thus standard interpretation, is impossible and always poses itself as an ideal. This is particularly true in the reading of poetry—still truer in the case of Chinese poetry in which the rhetorical progression is often alogical and the syntax ambiguous. It is hardly surprising to find that many translations of the same poem sometimes come out as totally different poems to the readers.[3]

Such being the case, "adequate comprehension" should mean, therefore, the translator's preliminary understanding of the language of the text, his awareness of its formalities, its rhetorical structure, and its syntactical peculiarities; and "adequate manipulation" of the medium should mean his awareness of its possibilities and limitations to approximate the structure of the original, whether or not he totally comprehends the poem in the text. I deem it important to add the last clause here, for it is quite possible (in fact, quite a few translators have already proved it) that the translator might comprehend the *text* adequately without comprehending much *poetry* in it. This is why the third part, "what happens in between," with which Mr. Fang has declined to deal himself, plays an even more important role. Here the translator begins to assume the title of a critic-poet.

With the "poem" comprehended or intuited from the given text and with the laws and limitations of the medium well in mind, the translator is ready to perform the transmission. He must decide which are the essential parts of the poem that

[3] See, for instance, the handy, though not up-to-date, edition of English translations of Chinese poetry (*Ying-hua-chi*, reprinted in Taipei, Taiwan, 1959) in which the editor took pains (and pleasure, no doubt) to put together the sometimes extremely diversified versions of the same poem with the original Chinese at the head. See also Roy Earl Teele's important book *Through A Glass Darkly* (Ann Arbor, 1949) in which one will find similar comparisons.

9

have to be preserved even at the expense of violating the medium and which parts of the text can be pared away or modified to suit the laws of the medium without destruction to either. There are, indeed, moments when the "poem" (dictated by the text) and the medium (dictated by usage) coincide, resulting in the happiest transmission. But such moments are rare and a godsend. That is why, in a special sense, translation can be said to be more difficult than actual composition. A poet no doubt meets the same dilemma in which he has to make a compromise between what is to be transmitted and the medium. However, he has no obligation to be faithful to this initial idea of the "poem." In fact, the finished work is often not the initial idea, but something quite different from its original conception. In the case of the translator, such freedom of imaginative flight is not permitted because the contour of the "poem" is much more clearly defined, having been "framed" in the text. If the translator is serious enough to be the agent of transmission, he should not alter the "poem" (though grasped from a personal viewpoint) to the degree that it no longer resembles that which is given in the text. This should not sound specific to any reader, for, do not all the translators claim that they have been faithful to the text? And yet take this early example by John Francis Davis:

See how the gently falling rain
Its vernal influence sweetly showers,
As though the calm and tepid eve
It silently bedews the flowers:

Cloudy and dark th'horizon spreads,
—Save where some boat its light is burning:
But soon the landscape's tints shall glow
All radiant, with morn returning.[4]

The original, in word-for-word translation, is:

[4] *Poeseos Sinensis Commentarii*, or *The Poetry of the Chinese.*
(Macao, 1834), p. 55.

10

Good rain know time season
with spring then start occur
follow wind sneak into night
moist thing slender no noise
wild path cloud all dark
river boat light alone bright
morning see red wet place
flower heavy Brocade City[5]

Or compare this recent example, the first four lines of a Tu Fu poem, rendered by Professor H. T. Lee, a distinguished scholar of Chinese literature, according to the biographical note at the end of his *The Story of Chinese Culture* (Taipei, Taiwan, 1964) from which these lines are taken (p. 115):

Crumbling away is the vast empire,
But the rivers and mountains as fresh and green as ever!
Deep in the Spring,
The city lies hidden amidst of towering trees
Luxuriant with green foliage.
Bemoaning of the receding of the Spring tide,
The flowers burst into tears of pink and red.
Lamenting over a sad separation,
The birds are crying their hearts out.

The original gives us only these words:

country broken mountain river exist
city spring grass tree deep
feel time flower splash tear
sad separate bird startle heart.

Between Davis and Lee there are many such unimaginable

---

[5] This word-for-word transcription and all subsequent ones are provided for the discussion of particular problems implied by the syntax. It goes without saying that the poetry in a poem often goes beyond the dictionary meanings of separate words. For concrete examples of this view, see Chapter III.

deviations from the original, made by scholars and poets alike who have considerable claim to scholarship and knowledge of both the Chinese and the English languages. The core of the problem, it seems to me, concerns not so much their ignorance of the text as it is their failure, as translators, to see the special mode of representation of reality constituted or made possible by the peculiarity of the Chinese language itself. If they had given primary consideration to the linguistic structure of the line, they probably would not have been carried away so easily from the original. In fact, as we shall see later, most of the successful translations seem to reflect this emphasis.

What is this unique mode of representation, implied in the poetics of the Chinese and made possible by the peculiarity of the Chinese language? Let me use a concrete example, "Taking Leave of a Friend" (Li Po),[6] which I will lay out in the most literal way possible, giving first the original (arranged horizontally from left to right for the sake of convenience); second, a word-for-word translation; third, a version almost as literal as the second but with elements introduced to make it English. These elements will be put in brackets to retain the sense of the syntax.

青　山　橫　北　郭
白　水　繞　東　城
此　地　一　為　別
孤　蓬　萬　里　征
浮　雲　遊　子　意

---

[6] The same example has been used by Mr. Teele in his *Through a Glass Darkly* (p. 34), for a different purpose. I choose this example rather than many thousands of others in order to prepare for the discussion of Pound's version.

12

green	mountain(s)	lie-across	north	outer-wall-of-city
white	water	wind-around	east	city
this	place	once	make	separation
lone	tumbleweed	ten-thousand	miles	travel
floating	cloud(s)	wanderer		thought (mood)
setting	sun	old	friend	feeling
wave	hand(s)	from	here	go
hsiao	*hsiao**	parting	horse	neigh

* onomatopoeic words for neighing.

Green mountain(s) lie across (the) north wall.
White water wind(s) (the) east city.
Here once (we) part,
Lone tumbleweed(;) (a) million miles (to) travel.
Floating clouds (;) (a) wanderer('s) mood.
Setting sun(;) (an) old friend('s) feeling.
(We) wave hands(,) (you) go from here.
Neigh, neigh goes (the) horse at parting.

This is a five-character regulated poem (*wu-lü*). Since, except in rare cases, there is practically no enjambment in Chinese poetry, each line is almost always a sentence, or, to avoid confusion, a group of words of completed meaning. Now in the five-character lines, the structure of each sentence can be understood in terms of the combinations of characters by which the meaning patterns are formed.[7] One common structure is: (1) 2-1-2

[7] See also the somewhat scientific classifications in Wang Li's *Han-yü Shih-lü-hsüeh* (*The Prosody of Chinese Poetry*, Shanghai, 1962), pp. 182-287. The book can perhaps be called also *The Poetics of Chinese Poetry*, since it discusses rhetoric as well as sentence structure. In

13

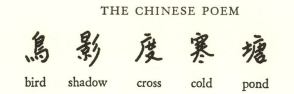

bird   shadow   cross   cold   pond

The middle character is usually a connective (verb, preposition, or adjective which assumes somewhat the character of a verb) to tighten the relation between the units before and after it. This structure most resembles the English subject-verb-object relation and thus the relation between the two units is often quite clear, grammatically speaking, although there are occasionally cases in which this middle connective can be very delusive, as in the line,

new   moon   move   gold   wave

Here we are not certain whether it is because of the lunar influence that the golden waves move or that the golden waves are seen moving as the new moonlight shows them.[8]

---

spite of the great number of lines analyzed there, one will find the result, obviously influenced by the Western frame of grammatical structure, sometimes proves to be detrimental to the understanding of Chinese poetry.

[8] This is a rather good line in which to show how ambiguity can enrich the poetic effect. But such ambiguity is almost untranslatable. At this point, perhaps we can experiment with Emily Dickinson's peculiar punctuation. In her poem, "There's a certain Slant of Light," we find these lines:

> Heavenly Hurt, it gives us—
> We can find no scar.
> But internal difference,
> Where the Meanings, are—
> None may teach it—Any—
> 'Tis the Seal Despair—

Before Thomas H. Johnson restored Dickinson's original punctuation,

As we can see now, the structure of the first two lines of "Taking Leave of a Friend" belong to this first type of sentence. Their correspondence to the English subject-verb-object structure has led our translators to render them into English without making any essential change in the structure from the original:

Pound (1915):
Blue mountains to the north of the walls,
White river winding about them;

P, 137

F. Ayscough-Amy Lowell (1921):
Clear green hills at a right angle to the North wall.
White water winding to the East of the city.[9]

Obata (1922):
Blue mountains lie beyond the north wall;
Round the city's eastern side flows the white water.[10]

---

the other published versions had the fifth line modified as "None may teach it anything." This shows how hard it is to decide the role of the dangling "Any." As it is now, it could very well mean "Any may teach it." Similarly, in the lines (in "Dare you see a Soul *at the White Heat?*")

Then crouch within the door—
Red—is the Fire's common tint—

"Red" is, no doubt, the predicate of "the Fire's common tint," but, separated by two dashes, it also refers somewhat to the previous line. Can we, then, apply this principle, if we can call it principle, to the Chinese line?

New moon—stirring—gold waves
(moving)

However, I do not mean to recommend it as the only way to translate, but it is instructive to see the problem involved here.

[9] *Fir-Flower Tablets* (New York, 1921) p. 50. "At a right angle to" is not correct in meaning, but as far as the "subject-connective-object" structure is concerned, it is closer than Giles, for instance. See examples following.

[10] *The Works of Li Po* (New York, 1922) p. 94.

15

And yet with Giles, Bynner (aided by Kiang Kang-hu, a learned Chinese scholar), and Judith Gautier, of whom Arthur Waley spoke approvingly,[11] this simple structure is destroyed.

Giles (1898):
    Where blue hills cross the northern sky,
      Beyond the moat which girds the town,
    'Twas there we stopped to say Goodbye![12]

Bynner (1920):
    With a blue line of mountains north of the wall,
    And east of the city a white curve of water,
    Here you must leave me and drift away . . .[13]

Gautier (1901):
    Par la verte montagne aux rudes chemins, je vous
      reconduis jusqu'à l'enceinte du Nord.
    L'eau écumante roule autour des murs, et se perd
      vers l'orient.[14]

What is lost in the destruction of the original structure is obvious, discounting Giles' unjustified change of "wall" to "sky" in order to rhyme with "Goodbye" in the third line and Gautier's addition of explanatory details that are not in the Chinese. In the original, or in the translations that observe the original structure, we see things in nature, very much like the objects in a painting, working upon us, while in Giles and Bynner and in Gautier's interpretive procedure, we are *led* to these things by way of intellectual, directional devices ("Where" "With"). We see the process of analysis at work rather than the things acting themselves out before us.

The fact that some of these Chinese lines are void of syn-

11 "Bibliographical Notes" in *170 Chinese Poems*, 3rd printing (New York, 1925), p. 35.
12 *Chinese Poetry in English Verse* (London, 1898), p. 70.
13 *Jade Mountain* (New York, 1920), p. 57.
14 *Revue de Paris* (Paris, 1901), 812.

tactical directives becomes much clearer when we come to examine the next type of structure: (2) 2-3.

There are many variations in this type of structure. Let us first look at some examples in which syntax does not become a problem. These are:

a. when the line tends to be conversational and free from the obligation of strict parallelism, as in:

獨	鶴	歸	何	晚
lone	crane	return	how	late

昏	鴉	己	滿	林
evening	crows	already	fill	forest

(A. C. Graham's translation:
How late the solitary crane returns!
But the twilight crows already fill the forest).[15]

The last three characters form the predicate (in the English sense) of the subject represented by the first two characters.

b. When reduplications are present, as in the last line of "Taking Leave of a Friend"

蕭	蕭	班	馬	鳴
neigh	neigh	parting	horse	neigh

(*Neigh, neigh* goes the horse at parting)

in which "neigh, neigh" is a quality about the action (or state) of the last three characters; or in the line

---

[15] *An Anthology of Chinese Literature*, eds., C. Birch and D. Keene (New York, 1965), p. 238.

17

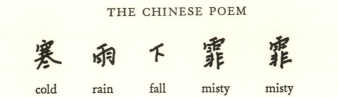

寒	雨	下	霏	霏
cold	rain	fall	misty	misty

in which the last three characters show the appearance of the cold rain falling.

But these syntactically rather clear lines are not as numerous as the following types which dominate the five-character poems:

[	A	]	[	B	]
noun	*verb*	*noun*	*noun*	*verb/adj*

國 破 山 河 在
城 春 草 木 深

Empire (is) broken (:) mountains and rivers remain.
Spring (in) city (:) grass and trees (grow) thick.[16]

Our translators give us these versions:

W.J.B. Fletcher (1933):
A nation though fallen, the land yet remains.
When spring fills the city, its foliage is dense.[17]

Edna W. Underwood (1929):
The country is broken—Nothing but mountains and hills.
When spring comes back to the city, the trees and the grasses grow green.[18]

[16] See also these same lines quoted earlier in this chapter.
[17] *More Gems of Chinese Poetry* (Shanghai, 1933), p. 96.
[18] *Tu Fu, Wanderer and Minstrel under Moons of Cathay* (Portland, Maine, 1929), p. 12.

William Hung (1952):
The country is shattered. Only the landscape remains.
Spring in the city? Yes, unpruned trees and over-
grown weeds.[19]

What is the relation between Group A and Group B, syntactically speaking? Is it true that one clause is subordinate
to the other, as both Fletcher and Underwood (as well as
Jenyns and Bynner)[20] have it? Apparently, the two are in a
paratactical relation, thus the approximation by Hung. And
yet, Hung finds it too abrupt to leave the two groups stand-
ing all by themselves without some kind of connection. Accordingly, he sneaks in the word "only" in the first line and
a "?" and the colloquial "yes" in the second line, and so re-
introduces the relation (syntactical commitment), changing
the basic mode of the original presentation. One would even
ask why the "?" is there at all. Again, this is analysis at work,
not the drama of things. The fact is that, in the original, the
two phases of perception, like two cones of light, cut into one
another simultaneously. Any attempt to re-connect them even
syntactically will destroy the simultaneity and fall back on the
logic of succession. This is Fletcher, Underwood, Bynner, and
Jenyns and, in a lesser degree, Hung. It looks rather hopeless
and most readers will eventually place the blame on the
English language itself. And yet, it is justified to translate

[*noun*   *verb*]   [*adj*   *noun*   *verb*]

Stars come: ten thousand houses move.

into "While the stars are twinkling above the ten thousand

---

[19] *Tu Fu: China's Greatest Poet* (Cambridge, Mass., 1952), p. 105.
[20] See *Selections from the Three Hundred Poems of the T'ang
Dynasty* (London, 1940), p. 98, and *Jade Mountain*, p. 148.

households . . ." (Hung, p. 125). Besides the deviation from the original structure, notice also the intellectual directive "while." Or these two lines

Stars dangle: flat plain broadens.
Moon surges: big river flows.

into

The stars lean down from open space.
And the moon comes running up the river.

> Bynner, p. 152

or

Stars drawn low by the vastness of the plain
The moon rushing forward in the river's flow.

> Birch, pp. 238-89

It is not that these images are not beautiful in themselves; the problem is whether or not we should preserve the original mode of apprehension or representation. From a critical viewpoint, how much are we entitled to allow the process of analysis to interfere with this somewhat strange and vigorously unanalytical presentation? The problem becomes even more pertinent in the next two variations of this structure:

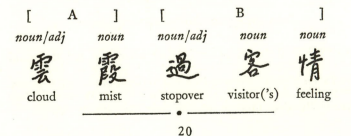

浮	雲	遊 于	意
floating	cloud(s)	wanderer('s)	thought(mood)

落	日	故	人	情
setting	sun	old	friend('s)	feeling

The structure of all three lines—the first line from Tu Fu
and the second two lines from "Taking Leave of a Friend"—
is exactly the same. I suppose most readers would easily take
Group A to be a qualification of Group B, but how? In the
first line, does it mean syntactically "Clouds and mists *are* a
sojourner's feeling [i.e. A sojourner's feeling *is* clouds and
mists]" or "Clouds and mists *are like* a sojourner's feeling
[A sojourner's feeling *is like* clouds and mists]"? The answer: it does and it does not at the same time. No reader
will fail to find the resemblance of a sojourner's feeling to the
transitoriness of the clouds and mists. And yet there is a flash
of interest in the syntactically uncommitted resemblance which
the introduction of the *verbs* (thus making it a metaphor) and
the word *like* (thus making it a simile) destroys easily. It can
be expected that this particular linguistic aspect would disturb
the translators of the second two lines of the same structure.
Let us see some of the translator's interpretations and effort
to retain this flash of interest.

> Your heart was full of wandering thought;
> For me,—my sun has set indeed;

This is Giles (p. 70), once hailed by Arthur Waley for
having combined "rhyme and literalness with wonderful dex-
terity."[21] Waley's praise does not seem to hold here. The

[21] In spite of the fact that he and Giles had a bitter argument over
the principle of translation in *New China Review* (February 1920-

counterpoint rhythm of the two visual images has entirely vanished.

> Mind like a floating wide cloud,
> Sunset like the parting of old acquaintances

This is Pound (1915).[22] The original juxtaposition of the two relatively concrete images is skillfully changed. Here an abstract idea is placed against a concrete image, forming an interest no less poetic than the original one. In fact, one can perhaps argue for Pound. Since it is the "thought (of the wanderer)" that is being juxtaposed with "floating clouds," he can drop the "wanderer" image and its suppression can be justified, so to speak, by the words "floating" (the movement of the wanderer) and "wide" (the space the wanderer is constantly to cover). However, we must understand that although, grammatically speaking, we may explain "thought" as the proper object juxtaposed with "floating clouds," the visual order is not to be violated, for it is in the *body* of the wanderer that the thought (or mood) is revealed and we actually see the *floating clouds* and the *wanderer* (and the state of mind he is in) *simultaneously*. Such a resemblance induced by a simultaneous presence of two objects can perhaps be best explained by the cinematic technique of montage. The effect of the montage, "the juxtaposition of two separate shots by splicing them together," says Sergei M. Eisenstein in his *The Film Sense*[23] (p. 7), "resembles not so much a simple sum of one shot plus another shot—as it does a *creation*. It resembles a creation—rather than a sum of its parts—from the circumstance that in every such juxtaposition *the result is*

November 1922). This remark appears in his *170 Chinese Poems*, 3rd printing, p. 35.

[22] Whether or not the Fenollosa notebooks contain the word "like" is at present unknown. Judging from the materials now available, the word "like" is probably not there.

[23] Tran. Jay Leyda (New York, 1942). See also pp. 4, 35.

qualitatively distinguishable from each component element viewed separately." In fact, Pound himself has given us the most searching explanation of this particular quality long before Eisenstein announced his own. In 1914 in his essay "Vorticism,"[24] he examines a *hokku* (*haiku*) composed by a Japanese naval officer. The hokku runs:

> The footsteps of the cat upon the snow:
> (are like) plum-blossoms.

Pound explains: "The words 'are like' would not occur in the original, but I add them for clarity. The 'one image poem' is a form of super-position,[25] that is to say, it is one idea set on top of another." Pound then switches to his composition of "In a Station of the Metro" in which he aptly takes away the words "is like":

> The apparition of these faces in the crowd:
> Petals, on a wet, black bough.

Again, in 1915, in an essay in the *New Age* which was later included in *Gaudier-Brzeska: A Memoir*, he discourses marvelously on this curious beauty:

> The pine-tree in the mist upon the far hill looks like a fragment of Japanese armour.
> The beauty of this pine-tree in the mist is not caused by its resemblance to the plates of the armour.
> The armour, if it be beautiful at all, is not beautiful *because* of its resemblance to the pine in the mist.
> In either case the beauty, in so far as it is beauty of form, is the result of 'planes in relation.'
> The tree and the armour are beautiful because their diverse planes overlie in a certain manner. (p. 167)

[24] *Fortnightly Review*, xcvi (September 1, 1914), 471. Reprinted in *GB*, 94-109.
[25] See Earl Miner's excellent discussion of this form in his *The Japanese Tradition in British and American Literature* (Princeton, 1958), pp. 112-23.

"Planes in relation" and "planes overlie in a certain manner" provide a perfect footnote to the kind of structure we have been talking about. Just why Pound did not try to bring out this juxtaposed effect in his translation of these two lines is not immediately relevant to the major concern of this chapter and I shall have occasion to return to it.

The peculiar flash of interest induced by the simultaneous presence of two objects is now obvious and it seems unnecessary to comment that the following versions of these same lines are all interpretive, each in its own way (except perhaps Obata's whose failure is of another kind):

> Les nuages légers flânent paresseusement, comme
> mes pensées.
> Bientôt le soleil se couche, et je sens, plus vivement
> encore,
> > la tristesse de la separation.
> > > Gautier (1901)

> Those floating clouds are like the wanderer's heart,
> Yon sinking sun recalls departed days.
> > Fletcher (1933)

> The floating clouds wander everywhither as does man.
> Day is departing—it and my friend.
> > Ayscough-Lowell (1921)

> I shall think of you in a floating cloud;
> So in the sunset think of me.
> > Bynner (1920)

> Oh, the floating clouds and the thoughts of a wanderer!
> Oh, the sunset and the longing of an old friend!
> > Obata (1928)

So far, the examples of the 2-3 structure we have seen are those which allow a free interpretation between the two halves of the line. Although we say the relation between them is syntactically uncommitted, some sort of relation is implied, otherwise our commentators and translators would not dare

24

to advance an interpretive relation (sometimes shamelessly personal) without feeling guilty. The next example we are to examine indicates a further step from the cinematic aspect we have already considered. The line "floating clouds; a wanderer's thought," involves a process of interiorization of the external objects. But the following lines are entirely surface manifestations:

noun	noun	noun	noun	noun
cock	crow	thatch	inn	moon
man	trace	wood	bridge	frost

These are selected details ("luminous details" that Ezra Pound once spoke of in another context?),[26] objects in their purest form uncontaminated by intellect or subjectivity. We know from these details that this is early morning and a trip is involved. These details are given to us at one instant to constitute an atmosphere that strongly suggests the actuality of the situation, but we can never be certain as to where, in the background, we should put the cock, the moon, the bridge. Are we to visualize these in the following manner: (At) cockcrow, the moon (is seen above) the thatched inn; footprints (are seen upon) the frost (covering) the wooden bridge? There are other ways of locating these details; for instance, the moon need not be "above" the inn, it could very well be just barely seen above the horizon.

We remember here that Walter Pater once, in defining the *Anders-streben* in art, talked about "some momentary con-

[26] "I Gather the Limbs of Osiris," *New Age*, x (December 7, 1911), 130.

junction of mirrors and polished armour and still water, by which all sides of a solid image are exhibited at once, solving that casuistical question whether painting can present an object as completely as sculpture." The ideal poetry, he continues, should be "exquisite pauses of time" arrested so that "we seem to be spectators of all the fullness of existence."[27] The analogy is not entirely exact, but this much is at least legitimate: these Chinese lines, like the shots in the movies and the montage technique, have touched upon the realms of painting and sculpture, although, unlike the movies, the objects are projected only on the screen of imagination, not literally before our eyes.

But excitement is bound to lapse into despair when we try to recapture in English the exact layout of the details in these Chinese lines. We will find conventional English quite ineffectual. Some kind of invention seems to be in demand, for, as we now see, the literalness of the Chinese line and the peculiar syntax in it have a claim upon us that no translator can afford to ignore.[28] It is no small wonder, therefore, to find that Arthur Waley (whose much-praised translations have set the mode for later translators to give the Chinese a fluid, logical, and grammatical surface) should be the very first one to approximate the structure of the Chinese line, an experiment he immediately abandoned. The following two examples are from his *Chinese Poems* (London, 1916):[29]

[27] "The School of Giorgione" in *Renaissance* (London, 1922), pp. 134, 149-50.
[28] Even without going over all other variations of the five-character and the more complicated seven-character lines, the sense of syntactical pecularity seems to be too obvious to need further demonstration.
[29] Waley never reprinted these poems in his well-known *170 Chinese Poems* or in his other translations. The ones of the same structural approximations reprinted in *170 Chinese Poems* were all modified into syntactically clear sentences. Compare, for example, "The Ejected Wife"

Yellow dusk: messenger fails to appear (p. 10)

The Chinese goes:

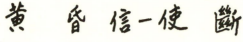

(yellow   dusk   messenger   broken)

The approximation is even more marked in these lines of a seven-character poem:

> In her boudoir, the young lady—unacquainted
>   with grief
> Spring day,—best clothes, mounts shining tower. (p. 9)

(1916) and the version in *170 Chinese Poems* (1918) (retitled "The Rejected Wife"):

> Entering the Hall, she meets the new wife;
> Leaving the gate, she runs into former husband.
> Words stick; does not manage to say anything.
> Presses hands together: stands hesitating.
> Agitates moon-like fan, sheds pearl-like tears,
> Realizes she loves him as much as ever—
> Present pain never come to an end.   (1916)

> Entering the Hall, she meets the new wife;
> Leaving the gate, she runs into *her* former husband.
> Words stick: *she* does not manage to say anything:
> *She* presses her hands together *and* hesitates.
> Agitates moon-like fan—sheds pearl-like tears
> Realizes she loves him as much as ever:
> *That* her present pain will never come to an end.

(Italics mine)

Notice how he inserts words to make the lines more grammatical and to break up the phases of perception that his earlier version has approximated.

It is intriguing to find that he agreed at such a late date (1965), just before he died, to reprint this little pamphlet which had been available, according to F. A. Johns, to only a few persons, among them Binyon, Eliot, Pound. (See "Notes" to *Chinese Poems* reprinted in 1965 by F. A. Johns). Did he mean to show some later translators and poets, including Pound, that he was actually the first person to use this method?

The Chinese, to use Fenollosa's word-for-word translation which seems correct enough in this case (see Appendix I), runs:

閨	中	少	婦	不	知	愁
Woman's-room	inside	young	wife	not	knew	sorrow

春	日	凝	粧	上	翠	樓
Spring	day	carefully-making	toilet	ascends	green-painted	storied-house

I need not point out the sharp resemblance of Waley's approximation to the literal structure of the original.

Another attempt is represented by Florence Ayscough in her translation in *Travels of a Chinese Poet, Tu Fu, Guest of Rivers and Lakes* (1934). Earlier she had done some T'ang poetry with the collaboration of Amy Lowell. This is the *Fir-Flower Tablets* (1921), examples of which we have already seen. In spite of the much-publicized and notorious "split-up" method linked with Pound's ideogrammic idea, the *Fir-Flower Tablets* was considered readable (at least in terms of the "modes" of Chinese translation at her time). The credit should go to Amy Lowell who managed to give the poems an up-to-date rhetoric. But her translations of Tu Fu which she undertook by herself are a complete failure. And yet, after three decades, A. C. Graham, with the same obsession with structural approximation as Ayscough's, has actually taken over her suggestion and has produced some rather successful versions. Let us look at a poem translated both by Ayscough and Graham. For the sake of convenience, the line structures are placed within brackets next to each literal Chinese line. The mark " ~ " means parataxis or "uncommitted relation."

clear	autumn	gaze	no	limit	$(2 \sim 3)$
distant	far	rise	layer	darkness	$(2 - 3)$
distant	water	connect	sky	clean	$(2\text{-}1\text{-}2) \; / \; (2\text{-}2\text{-}1)$
lone	city	lurk-in	mist	deep	$(2\text{-}1\text{-}2) \; / \; (2\text{-}2\text{-}1)$
leaf	scarce	wind	still	drop	$(2 \sim 3)$
mountain	wind(v.)	sun	first	sink	$(2 \sim 3)$
lone	crane	return	how	late	$(2 - 3)$
evening	crows	already	fill	forest	$(2 - 3)$

Ayscough (p. 36):

Limpid	autumn;	I gaze,	no	limit;
Remote,	far-off,	rise	layers	of darkness.
Distant	waters	bird	with cold	sky;
Lone	city	blurs	in deep	mist,
Sparse	leaves	through wind,	still, further	drop;
Divided	peaks	through lack	of sun,	dulled.
Single	crane	returns home	at which	sinking of the sun?
Hour of	yellow dusk;	trees	brimful	of rooks.

A. C. Graham (Birch, p. 238):

Clear autumn, sight has no bounds;
High in the distance piling shadows rise.
The farthest waters merge in the sky unsullied;
A neglected town hides deep in mist.
Sparse leaves, which the wind still sheds.
Fall hills, where the sun sinks down.
How late the solitary crane returns!
But the twilight crows already fill the forest.

Ayscough's failure is too obvious to need comment. Besides misinterpretations at various places which I need not elaborate upon, the language is clumsy and unintelligible. Yet notice the similarity in structure between Graham and Ayscough and between them and the original. On the whole, Graham has observed both the parataxis (line 1) and syntax (lines 2, 3, 4, 7, 8) as well as the visual order,[30] although in lines 5 and 6 he has changed slightly the paratactical relations.

[30] The same is true in his book of translations *Poems of the Late T'ang* (Baltimore, 1965) in which many excellent lines show this

What this comparison aims to show is that it is not entirely impossible in English, within limits, to observe the literal structure and yet achieve the transmission of poetry. Graham's version is, in many ways, superior to William Hung's interpretive translation:

I look at the endless expanse of the limpid autumn; A few layers of mist rise in the horizon. The distant river carries away the clear sky. A lonely city is blurred by the thick smoke from a thousand hearths. The wind tears more leaves from the thinning trees; Behind the hills far away, the sun has sunk. That single crane is rather late on its return flight; The forest is already full of roosting crows.

Hung, p. 152

The third kind of approximation is represented by C. H. Kwock and Vincent McHugh's collaboration. We remember from the above examples that in translating Chinese poetry into English, we are forced to insert "connectives" (ranging from conjunctions like "when," "while," "though," prepositions like "in," "above," "like," to verbs "is," "are," etc.), to make good sense in English, thus incurring a loss which I have already explained. Here is an effort to take away these "insertions," though perhaps at the expense of the destruction of the original line-length. The seven-character line is rendered this way:

City of Wei
the morning rain
wet
on light dust

Birch, p. 224

which has been translated in the conventional mode as:

---

observation of sentence structure. This book also contains a good discussion of what might be called post-Empsonian directions in translation.

The morning rains *of* Wei Ch'eng moisten the light
dust.   Jenyns, p. 39

A morning-rain has settled the dust *in* Wei-ch'eng.
                                        Bynner, p. 191

The morning rain *of* Wei City wets the white dust.
                        Li Fu-ning in *White Pony*, ed.,
                        R. Payne (London, 1947), p. 153
                                        (All italics mine)

Here is a five-character line:

Sky still blue
        not a rag of cloud
                                        Birch, p. 226

which, in the hands of Bynner and Fletcher, runs:

There is not one cloud in the whole blue sky.
                                        Bynner, p. 58

No cloud to fleck the spotless sky *that stretches mile
on mile.*
                                Fletcher, *Gems*, p. 34

All these other translations have, of course, followed the
original line-length, i.e., one English line for one Chinese
line, but they have no claim to structural approximation nor
to the observation of the visual order of the images.

At this point, readers familiar with modern English and
American poetry are apt to ask: do not all these attempts,
including Waley's miscarried effort, remind us of Pound's
later poetry or the poetry that has been largely influenced by
Pound's language in the *Cantos*? Did not Pound once approximate an ancient Chinese poem in his Canto 49:

Sun up; work
sundown; to rest
dig well and drink of the water
dig field; eat of the grain
imperial power is? and to us what it is?

31

The Chinese of this Canto, word-for-word, runs:

sun	rise	*particle**	work
sun	down	*particle**	rest
dig	well	*particle**	drink
till	field	*particle**	eat
imperial power to us what have/is *particle***			

---

* A functional word to link the two halves of a line. It does not have a definite meaning, and can mean, in different contexts, "and," "yet," "also," "but," "nevertheless," "like" and "as." In fact, many sinologists argue that such particles should not be translated at all.

** This second particle, different from the first one, functions as an interrogative or exclamatory ending.

Indeed, one may continue, does not the rest of the Canto, obviously constructed out of scraps of Chinese poetry, contain a structural peculiarity that strongly resembles the Chinese lines?[31]

However, to attribute this invention to Pound seems quite unwarranted. Not only does Waley's example (though he abandoned it for fear of its strangeness) date from before Pound's practice, but we must not forget that Pound, on the whole, did not wholeheartedly employ the described methods in his translations of the *Cathay* poems. Pound's language, in particular his paratactical structures and line divisions stems from a poetics which develops from his early poems through *Cathay* to the *Cantos*; we will examine this development in the following chapters. For the time being, this much we can perhaps say: Out of this poetics—the language that he developed which has consequently been followed and modified by other American poets, notably Williams, Olson, Creeley, and Snyder[32]—it has been possible for translators to put back

[31] For example the lines "Rain; empty river; a voyage," "Broad water; geese line out with the autumn" and many similar examples throughout the *Cantos*.

[32] Gary Snyder, who actually studied Chinese at the University of California at Berkeley, displayed the most conscious approximation of the Chinese syntax. See particularly the poem, "Eight Sandbars on

into the translation of Chinese poetry the same degree of readers' participation and the same exercise of imagination that the interpretive translations had taken out by replacing the dramatic with the analytical mode of representation.

---

the Takano River" in which the first line is spaced out as five line-units, vertically like the Chinese line:

well water   I
cool in
summer
warm in
winter

with the numbers 1, 2, 3, etc. to indicate that the five line-units are to be taken as one line.

chapter two

Precision or Suggestion: Pre-*Cathay* Obsessions

1

In 1918, three years after the publication of *Cathay*, two install-ments of a short essay by Pound simply titled "Chinese Poetry" appeared in the little magazine *To-day*. For the first time since he had received Fenollosa's notebooks, he expressed in public his opinions on the translations he had made.[1] He begins this little known essay in a familiar manner: "It is because Chinese poetry has certain qualities of vivid presen-tation; and because certain Chinese poets have been content to set forth their matter without moralizing and without com-ment that one labours to make a translation."[2] These character-istics, namely "vivid presentation" and "without moralizing and without comment," echo, of course, the imagist credo: "Direct treatment of the thing" (Summer, 1912, *LE*, 3), "Don't be viewy" (1913, *LE*, 6), and many related points. These dicta are implicit in his "Prolegomena" of February 1912 which led to the imagist principles. In fact, the same dicta reach far back to his medieval studies in "I Gather the Limbs of Osiris" (1911) which, along with *The Spirit of Romance*

---

[1] Before this, Pound had only mentioned them in letters with exaltation, but no discussion. His short notice of Edgar Lee Masters in the *Egoist*, II (January 1, 1915), 11-12 in which he compares certain passages of the American poet to Li Po and to lines in "Song of the Bowmen of Shu," seems to me too tenuous to afford much insight into Chinese poetry.

[2] *To-day*, III (April 1918), 54.

(1910), derived from his Regent Street Polytechnic lectures[3] delivered in 1908 shortly after his arrival in London: "The artist seeks out the luminous detail and presents it. He does not comment."[4] The watchword for the entire *Spirit of Romance* is, no doubt, "vivid presentation." The earliest testimony is found in Pound's letter to William Carlos Williams of October 21, 1908, which contains these standards:

1. To paint the thing as I see it.
2. Beauty.
3. Freedom from didacticism . . . .[5]

But "vivid presentation" is a broad and general concept. What did Pound actually mean by it in or before 1914? What are the "certain qualities" that might correspond to aspects of Pound's poetic practice at that time? Some of the poems in *Cathay* certainly contain moralizing and commentary; what makes Pound claim that they are free from these defects? To answer these questions, we will have to examine the particular problems that had been stirring all these years in Pound's sensibility as poet and critic. Perhaps we can then see why some of the Chinese poems seemed to suit his temperament so well.

2

Many critics have argued that the core of Pound's criticism is his demand for precise visualization rather than suggestiveness. Herbert Newton Schneidau, for example, has summed up Pound's critical views in these clear-cut terms. He says:

He [Pound] formed his literary tastes on the principle of precise visualization: exalted Dante because of it, and demoted Milton (and even Shakespeare) because of the lack

---

[3] Charles Norman, *Ezra Pound* (New York, 1960), pp. 30-34. Cf. *SR*, 92: "Here the preciseness of description denotes, I think, a clarity of imaginative vision."
[4] *New Age*, x.6 (December 7, 1911), 130.
[5] *Letters*, 6.

of it. Several times in *The Spirit of Romance* Pound contrasted the methods of Dante and Shakespeare, and applied to their differing techniques two labels which were to become extremely important to him: "exact definition" and "vague suggestiveness." Dante's method, that of exact definition, of course, depended first on visualization, primary epithets,[6] precision and accuracy in reproduction. Suggestiveness, on the other hand, was the evocation of emotional effects through secondary epithets and vague, mysterious words . . . naturally this method uses inexactness and imprecision deliberately, and employs visualization only for sensuous ends, not accuracy. Pound eschewed the suggestive mode for himself, and "definition" became a hortatory term for him.[7]

He goes on to point out that all Pound's imagist principles—"precision," "concrete diction," "go in fear of abstraction," etc.—developed from this central obsession. Indeed, one can find supporting statements in Pound's critical writings in this period, particularly in "The Serious Artist" of 1913.[8]

But is it true that Pound had always tried to eschew "suggestiveness" and "vagueness"? And if so, would it not be strange to find him in the same essay on Chinese poetry advocating at once a poem "of great vigor and clarity" (i.e. "South-Folk in Cold Country") and a poem that requires readers to "puzzle over" it and "play Conan Doyle" (i.e. "The

---

[6] For a definition of the primary and secondary epithets, see subsequent pages.

[7] Herbert Newton Schneidau, *Ezra Pound's Criticism and the Influence of His Literary Relationships in London, 1908-1920* (Unpublished doctoral dissertation, Princeton University, 1962), p. 10.

[8] See also "Status Rerum" (December 10, 1912) in *Poetry*, I.4 (January 1913), 125-26; "[Mr. Yeats] has much in common with the French symbolists. Mr. Hueffer believes in an exact rendering of things. He would strip words of all "association" for the sake of getting a precise meaning . . . space forbids me to set forth the program of the *Imagistes* at length, but one of their watchwords is Precision."

Jewel Stairs' Grievance")? In fact, Pound was so much intrigued by the "game" that he decided to put the readers to the same kind of mental play by including the result at the end of the poem (and by repeating it in the same essay).

The problem, to be exact, is to see where Pound, as poet and critic, stood between the two poles of precision and suggestion, for Pound had never been a precisionist in the sense that he had eschewed the suggestive mode. We remember that even in "The Serious Artist," in which the dominant thesis is "precision," Pound had said: "You can be wholly precise in representing a vagueness. You can be wholly a liar in pretending that the particular vagueness was precise in its outline." (LE, 44). We also remember that Pound's "The Return," written one year earlier, does not depend on primary epithets; its visualization is of the kind whose outline is not clearly defined, and it evokes "emotional effects."

> See, they return; ah, see the tentative
> Movements, and the slow feet,
> The trouble in the pace and the uncertain
> Wavering!
>
> See, they return, one, and by one,
> With fear, as half-awakened;
> As if the snow should hesitate
> And murmur in the wind,
>   and half turn back;
> These were the "Wing'd-with-Awe,"
>   Inviolable.
>
> Gods of the winged shoe!
> With them the silver hounds,
>   sniffing the trace of air!
> Haie! Haie!
>   These were the swift to harry;
> These the keen-scented;
> These were the souls of blood.

Slow on the leash,
pallid the leash-men!

P, 74

There is nothing definite about these returning "men." Are they the ghosts of some heroes? Are they hunters? Or is it only as Patricia Hutchins tries to pinpoint it, the Masterman who "wavers from hope to caution and ends by saying that he cannot tell where we stand," a personification of the condition of England at that time?[9] And what is the relation of this poem to his early poem "Piere Vidal Old" (*P,* 30), in which we find the theme of men hunting Piere Vidal who ran mad, as a wolf, because of love, and in which we find this ending:

[*Sniffing the air*
Ha! this scent is hot!

Whatever it is, we are given but selected details in synecdochic form that build up, by suggestion, a state of ineffable emotion. Pound once described this type of representation as an "objective" image: "Emotion seizing upon some external scene or action carries it intact to the mind, and that vortex purges it of all save the essential or dominant qualities, and it emerges like the external original."[10] It is as if we are led to concentrate by the spotlight on a few shots—the slow feet, the wavering (body?), the winged shoe, the leash. The picture can only be completed within the reader's imagination, ignited by the emotionally intact (but not visually complete) details the poet presents.

Apparently, Pound's attitude as poet and critic was ambivalent. It seems that in spite of the fact that Pound laid paramount importance on words such as "precision" and "visual representation," he did not intentionally dismiss the "ineffable"

[9] Patricia Hutchins, *Ezra Pound's Kensington* (London, 1965), p. 100.
[10] "Affirmations. . . . iv. As for Imagisme," *The New Age,* xvi (January 28, 1915), 349.

or the "suggestive mode." Let us go back to the passage in *The Spirit of Romance* which gives rise to the thesis of Pound's precisionist stance.

If the language of Shakespear is more beautifully sugges-tive, that of Dante's is more beautifully definite; both men are masters of the whole art. Shakespear is perhaps more brilliant in his use of epithets of proper quality; thus I doubt if there be in Dante, or in all literature, any epithet so masterfully-placed as is Shakespear's in the speech of the Queen-mother to Hamlet, where she says: "And with the incorporal air do hold discourse," suggesting both the common void of the air which she sees and the ghostly form at which Hamlet stands aghast; on the other hand, Dante is, perhaps, more apt in "comparison."

"The apt use of metaphor, arising, as it does, from a swift perception of relations, is the hallmark of genius": thus says Aristotle. I use the term "comparison" to include metaphor, simile (which is a more leisurely expression of a kindred variety of thought), and the "language beyond metaphor," that is, the more compressed or elliptical expression of meta-phorical perception, such as antithesis suggested or implied in verbs and adjectives; for we find adjectives of two sorts, thus, adjectives of pure quality, as: white, cold, ancient; and adjectives which are comparative, as: lordly. Epithets may also be distinguished as epithets of primary and second-ary apparition. By epithets of primary apparition I mean those which describe what is actually presented to the sense or vision. Thus in *selva oscura*, "shadowy wood"; epithets of secondary apparition or after-thought are such as in "*sage* Hippotades" or "*forbidden* tree." Epithets of primary ap-parition give vividness to description and stimulate convic-tion in the actual vision of the poet. . . . There are also epithets of "emotional apparition," transensuous, suggestive: thus in Mr. Yeats' line: "Under a bitter *black* wind that

blows from the left hand." Dante's colouring and qualities
of the infernal air, although they are definitely symbolical
and not indefinitely suggestive, foreshadow this sort of
epithet. The modern symbolism is more vague, it is sometimes allegory in three dimensions instead of two, sometimes
merely atmospheric suggestion.

SR, 166-167

Although Pound seemed to favor the primary epithet, he did
not demote Shakespeare for being suggestive. He put Dante
and Shakespeare on the same level, and in fact, judging from
the sentence, "thus I doubt if there be in Dante, or in all literature, any epithet so masterfully-placed as is Shakespear's,"
we might even argue that, as far as presentation is concerned,
he sometimes regarded Shakespeare as greater than Dante.[11]
Nor should we consider his mention of Yeats' transensuous,
suggestive epithet of "emotional apparition" as derogatory.
When Pound exalted Dante's preciseness, he did not entirely
reject vagueness. "Dante's greater poetry rises above the age,
. . . because of the lofty, austere spirit moving behind the
verse. The spirit shows itself in the tangled canzone of the
'Convito'; an ode, I think . . . obscure, . . . at first reading;
but when the sense and form are once comprehended its
beauty is a beauty that never tires one." (*SR*, 100) And again,
"There are two kinds of beautiful painting. . . . One looks
at the first kind of painting and is immediately delighted by
its beauty; the second kind of painting, when first seen, puzzles
one, but on leaving it, and going from the gallery one finds
new beauty in natural things. . . . Thus, there are works of

[11] See also: "Here [in Guido Guinicelli's poetry] the preciseness of
the description denotes, I think, a clarity of imaginative vision. In
more sophisticated poetry an epithet would suffice, the picture would
be suggested. The dawn would be 'rosy-fingered' or 'in russet-clad'."
(*SR*, 92) Pound's poetry is, of course, of the sophisticated kind. Closer
study of Pound will show that the relation between Pound and Shakespeare is not as tenuous as most people think.

40

art which are beautiful objects and works of art which are keys or passwords admitting one to a deeper knowledge, to a finer perception of beauty; Dante's work is of the second sort." (*SR*, 162) Here Dante, as Pound understood him, is not merely a poet of primary epithets, but also a poet of subtle suggestion, whose power lies in offering *keys* "to a finer perception of beauty."

3

Pound's ambivalent position was complicated by the fact that his early poems—many of them contemporary with *The Spirit of Romance*—greatly belie his critical assertions. We find in these early poems an ethereal atmosphere, intangible shadows and light, obsessive symbols (jewels, opals, "gem-like" flame), semi-symbolic scenery (wind or wee-wind vaguely evoking dreamland), epithets of "emotional apparition" ("When the white hart breaks his cover/ And the white wind breaks the morn." *P*, 25) and more consciously intellectual symbols (e.g. the tree—the experience of metamorphosis).[12] None of these aspects can strictly be called precise rendering of the thing. We remember, in the Prologue to the *Kora In Hell: Improvisations* (1920), William Carlos Williams' record of Pound's practice in that period:

My parent [father] had been holding forth in downright sentences upon my "idle nonsense" when he turned and be-

[12] Many of these aspects have been studied first by N. Christoph de Nagy in his *The Poetry of Ezra Pound: The Pre-Imagist Stage* (Berne, Switzerland: The Cooper Monographs, 1960) and recently in greater detail by Hugh Witemeyer in his *Ezra Pound's Poetry 1908-1916* (Unpublished doctoral dissertation, Princeton University, 1966). Cf. "La Fraisne" (*P*, 4, *ALS*, 15), "Plotinus" (*ALS*, 56), "Masks" (*ALS*, 52), "Grace Before Song" (*ALS*, 13), "Beddoesque" (*ALS*, 104), "In Durance" (*P*, 20), "The White Stag" (*P*, 25), "The Flame" (*P*, 50), "Motif" (*ALS*, 73), "Song" (*ALS*, 72), "The Tree" (*P*, 3, *ALS*, 54). These traits pervade most of Pound's early poems. The examples I have listed are poems in which they are most prominent.

came equally vehement concerning something Ezra had written: what in heaven's name Ezra meant by "jewels" in a verse that had come between them. . . . Pound went on to explain with great determination and care, [that they] were the backs of books as they stood on a man's shelf. "But why in heaven's name don't you say so then?" was my father's triumphant and crushing rejoinder. (p. 13)

These roundabout ways of presenting poetic substance are, as we now understand, what Pound learned from the poets of the 'nineties and the early Yeats, as well as from the Aesthetic School.[13] In fact, Pound did not hesitate to acknowledge his debts to these poets in his essays and letters.[14] Among these acknowledgments, the statements that are of particular relevance to our discussion of Pound at this stage were made in his letter to René Taupin in 1928:

Rapports fr. > eng. via Arthur Symons etc., 1896. Baudelaire, Verlaine, etc. . . .

. . . l'idée de l'image doit "quelque chose" aux symbolistes français via T. E. Hulme, via Yeats < Symons < Mallarmé.
Letters, 216 and 218

The chart shows that certain aspects of Mallarmé and Verlaine had gone into the making of Pound's central consciousness. But what are these aspects? And since it was through Arthur Symons that Pound inherited these qualities, what was Symons' version of Mallarmé and Verlaine that appealed to Pound? If Verlaine represents the loosely termed impressionism[15] on the one hand and Mallarmé stands for symbolism on

---

[13] Eliot and Leavis were the earliest to point this out. For full studies of these influences on Pound's early poetry, see Nagy and Witemeyer.

[14] See particularly his "Prolegomena" (1912), *LE*, 11, "Lionel Johnson" (1915), *LE*, 367 and *Letters*, 216 and 218.

[15] Many critics called Verlaine an impressionist, for example, Symons and Strachey. See notes 22, 23, and 28.

the other, the problem becomes even more intriguing, because Pound openly dissociated himself from both camps (*GB*, 94-108).[16] Which aspect or aspects of either camp had Pound actually adopted and in what way? In order to answer these questions, recourse to definitions of these two movements as they originated in France would be of no use here. We have to return to the intermediary, Arthur Symons, to see the particular frame of mind in which he perceived these movements before we can see Pound in the right perspective.

4

Symons' version of Mallarmé and Verlaine is found in his influential book *The Symbolist Movement in Literature* (1899). But throughout the book he employed many key phrases that were already coined by Walter Pater in discussing Mallarmé and Verlaine. Especially marked is the repetition of Pater's concepts of the intense moment as a "gem-like flame" and life as flux, and his dictum "All art constantly aspires toward the condition of music."[17] We must, in turn, try to understand Symons in terms of a certain aspect of Pater.

In 1865, before his *Renaissance* was published, Pater noticed the shift of sensibility in modern man. He argued that, under the influence of the sciences of observation, modern thought cultivates the "relative" spirit in place of the "absolute." Whereas ancient thought sought "to arrest every object in an eternal outline," the modern spirit asserts that "nothing is, or can be rightly known except relatively and under conditions." As the physical conditions about man and man's organism become more and more complex, modern man becomes

. . . so receptive, all the influences of nature and of society ceaselessly playing upon him, so that every hour in his

[16] Discussion of this gesture will follow.
[17] Pound resorts to Pater's dictum in his essay on vorticism (*GB*, 94).

life is unique, changed altogether by a stray word, or glance, or touch. It is the truth of these relations that experience gives us, not the truth of eternal outlines ascertained once for all, but a world of fine gradations and subtly linked conditions, shifting intricately as ourselves change—and bids us, by a constant clearing of the organs of observation and perfecting of analysis, to make what we can of these. To the intellect, the critical spirit, just these subtleties of effect are more precious than anything else. What is lost in precision of form is gained in intricacy of expression.[18]

To be successful in life, Pater says in the Conclusion to *The Renaissance*, is to maintain the ecstasy, to dwell in every intense moment: "Not the fruit of experience, but experience itself, is the end." And he continues "to burn always with this hard, gem-like flame. . . . What we have to do is to be for ever curiously testing new opinions and courting new impressions, never acquiescing in a facile orthodoxy."[19]

This urge for the artist to let impressions play upon him and to grasp every moment for whatever it is easily led Symons to praise Verlaine the man with these words: "Verlaine was a man who gave its full value to every moment, who got out of every moment all that that moment had to give him."[20] And he described Verlaine the poet with these words (in spite of the fact that Pater disliked Verlaine's poetry):[21] "It is a twilight art, full of reticence, of perfumed shadows, of hushed melodies. It suggests, it gives impressions with a subtle avoid-

---

[18] "Coleridge," *Appreciations* (London, 1924), pp. 66-68.

[19] *The Renaissance* (London, 1922), pp. 236-37. Compare Yeats' opinion of the 'nineties poets: ". . . they wished to express life at its intense moments, these moments that are brief because of their intensity, and at those moments alone." ("Modern Poetry," *Essays and Introductions* [London, 1961], p. 464).

[20] *The Symbolist Movement in Literature*, p. 205.

[21] See "Walter Pater" in Symons' *Figures of Several Centuries* (London, 1916), p. 301.

44

ance of any too definite or precise effect of line or colour."[22] More than once, Symons quoted from Verlaine's "Art Poetique" the line *par la couleur, rien que la nuance* to define Verlaine's poetry.[23]

This is a superficial poetry, a poetry of moods, instinctive and temperamental in nature. At best, it is a kaleidoscopic array of clear images or of "luminous shadows" (*The Symbolist Movement in Literature*, p. 216), the interplay of light and shade, whose subtlety lies in *nuances* among these impressions. Symons himself gave us the best articulation of this type of poetry—the search for sensation through impressions:

> Night, a grey sea, a ghostly sea
> the soft beginning of rain . . .
>
> *Silhouettes*, "On the Beach"

and atmospheric visualization:

[22] "Notes on Paris and Paul Verlaine" in *Colour Studies in Paris* (London, 1918), pp. 171-72.

[23] It is interesting to note that Lytton Strachey, who disliked Symons and Yeats ("Modern Poetry" *Spectator*, 100, April 18, 1908, 622-23) should compare Herbert Giles' Chinese translations (from which Pound made a few adaptations) to Verlaine in these terms:

It [Chinese poetry] aims at producing an *impression*. . . . It *hints* at wonders. . . . [These poems] are like odours, for all their *intangibility*, the strange compelling powers of suggested reminiscence and romance. Whatever their subject, they remain *ethereal* . . . [these poets are] poets of reflection, preoccupied with patient beauties and *subtle* relationships of simple things . . . perhaps the Western writer whose manner they suggest most constantly is Verlaine. Like him, they know the art of being *quiet* in verse. Like him, they understand how the fluctuations of temperament may be reflected and accentuated by such outward circumstances.

"An Anthology," 1908, from *Characters and Commentaries* (New York, 1933), pp. 140-41.

(All italics mine)

While it is not certain if Pound held similar views on Giles' translations when he made from them a few adaptations, it should be pointed out here that much of Pound's pre-Cathay poetry reflect Strachey's description of Chinese poetry.

45

Miraculous silver-work in stone
Against the blue miraculous skies.
Silhouettes, "At Burgos"

In the moonlight room your face,
Moonlight-coloured, fainting white
Silhouettes, "Clair De Lune"[24]

But the aspect of Verlaine as understood by Symons is not a poetry of depth. That is why Yeats soon abandoned it and turned to symbolism; first to emotional symbols (what Pound calls epithet of "emotional apparition") which Pound adopted, and then to intellectual and esoteric symbols which Pound did not wholly pursue. That is why Pound in his letters denounced Verlaine and exalted Mallarmé.[25] The crux seems to lie in Pound's concern with the "method" of representation, just as Mallarmé is obsessed with Edgar Allan Poe's "precision and rigid consequence of a mathematical problem."[26] It is more than coincidence that Pound should define poetry as "a

[24] As Pound recalls it in his *Cantos*:
and with Symons remembering Verlaine at the Tabarin.
80/72
Serenely in the crystal jet as the bright ball that the
fountain tosses
(Verlaine) as diamond clearness.
74/27
But even in his late years, Pound employs an impressionism transformed (through a process which we can only elaborate in later chapters):
moon, cloud, tower, a patch of battistero
all of a whiteness.
79/62
[25] *Letters*, 23 (September 1913) ". . . there are few enough people who know anything beyond Verlaine and Baudelaire—neither of whom is the least use, pedagogically, I mean. They beget imitation and one can learn nothing from them." But in his letter to René Taupin, Pound linked Mallarmé with the idea of the image. (*Letters*, 218.)
[26] "The Philosophy of Composition," *Works*, xiv, 195.

46

sort of inspired mathematics" and "equations for the human emotions." (*SR*, 5) Pound's description—to use Mallarmé's words, "a series of unriddlings"—of "In a Station of the Metro" reminds one of Poe's unravelling of his "Raven," the conception of which Mallarmé greatly admired: "Plus j'irai, plus je serai fidèle a ces sévères idées que m'a léguées mon grand maître Edgar Poe. Le poème inoui du *Corbeau* à été ainsi fait. Et l'âme du lecteur jouit absolument comme le poète a voulu qu'elle jouit."[27]

One may argue here that because Pound openly dissociated himself from impressionism and symbolism (*GB*, 94-108), he should not be indebted to either. This is delusive. The curious thing about the process of influences is that two such fundamentally different movements as impressionism and symbolism (one being temperamental and external, the other, intellectual and internal) should come together under the same roof of symbolism in Symons' *The Symbolist Movement in Literature*. He gave us this explanation: "Impressionism and Symbolism are really working on the same hypothesis, applied in different directions. . . . The Impressionist . . . would flash upon you in a new, sudden way so exact an image of what you have just seen. . . . The Symbolist in this new sudden way, would flash upon you the 'soul' of that which can be apprehended only by the soul—the finer sense of things unseen, the deeper meaning of things evident."[28] The fact is that, stylistically speaking, both impressionism, including futurism which Pound calls "accelerated impressionism" (*GB*, 94), and symbolism have an easily discernible similarity in arrangement and presentation.

Impressionism, as represented by Symons' poetry, shows (in the first example quoted above) a *disconnectedness* in

[27] Guy Michaud, *Message Poétique du Symbolisme* (Paris, 1947, 3 vols.) I, 165. Compare also the unravelling process Pound attached to the Chinese poem "The Jewel Stairs' Grievance."

[28] "The Decadent Movement in Literature," *Harpers* (November 1893), 859.

style, the lines consisting mainly of nouns or several unconnected phrases, focusing on one distinctive feature of an object or event. The disconnectedness of style became part of
the manifesto of Marinetti's futurism. Pound must have had
this peculiar aspect in mind when he called futurism "accelerated impressionism." The manifesto reads: "Wireless Imagination . . . entire freedom of images and analogies expressed
by disjointed words and without the connecting wires of
syntax. . . . Poetry must be an interrupted sequence of new
images."[29] With these disconnected phases of perception there
is the inevitable sense of simultaneity, for the logic of sequence
is destroyed. It is as if every recorded moment were suspended
in time. The role each moment is to assume in the poem is
not clear until all other moments are present.

The stylistic features represented by Mallarmé are described
by Symons as follows: "Mallarmé is obscure, not so much
because he writes differently as because he thinks differently
from other people. His mind is elliptical . . . he emphasizes
the effect of what is unlike other people in his mind by
resolutely ignoring even the links of connection that exist
between them."[30] And later in the same essay:

> Imagine the poem already written down, at least composed.
> In its very imperfection, it is clear, it shows the links by
> which it has been riveted together; the whole process of
> construction can be studied. Now, most writers would be
> content; but with Mallarmé the work has only begun. In
> the final result there must be no sign of making. . . . Start
> with an enigma, and then withdraw the key of the enigma;
> and you arrive, easily, at the frozen impenetrability of those
> later sonnets.[31]

[29] *Poetry and Drama*, ed., Harold Monro, 1 (1913), 321. Marinetti's
own poetry is even more daringly explicit than the manifesto: "Sun
gold billets dishes lead sky/ silk heat bed quilting purple blue."
Whether it will stand as poetry is not our concern here.
[30] *The Symbolist Movement in Literature*, p. 181.
[31] *Ibid.*, pp. 197-98.

48

The fact that, stylistically, some of Pound's imagist poems, his Chinese adaptations, and much of the Cantos are similar to the above descriptions will become increasingly clear as we go on. This development is in tune with the credo of "freedom from didacticism" or "freedom from discursiveness" which he inherited from the Pre-Raphaelites. The attempt to eliminate the prose part in poetry by recording (or arranging) perception into several unconnected phases is but a further step toward the pure state of poetry.

Now Pound is essentially a poet of ideas, although he avoids setting forth his ideas in statements and indulges in images. He is not content with superficial impressions, and naturally he turns toward the poetry of depth or the poetry of intelligence. Like the symbolist, he is always concerned with turning external objects inward. Commenting upon his "In a Station of the Metro," he said, "In a poem of this sort one is trying to record the precise instant when a thing outward and objective transforms itself, or darts into a thing inward and subjective." (*GB*, 103) But, except in some of his early poems, Pound seldom practiced the first part of Mallarmé's principle: *that to name is to destroy, to suggest is to create.*[32] Nor did he adopt the "magic" or "mystic" position of the symbolist. (*GB*, 107: "The Vorticist movement is not a movement of mystication.") He does not rely on the Yeatsean mythological system for coherence and unity. How much, then, can he still be identified with impressionism and symbolism, and to what extent is he different from them? Let us turn to his criticism of these movements.

In 1912, in his "Prolegomena," Pound renounced impressionism[33] with these words: "The conception of poetry is a process more intense than the reception of an impression. And

---

[32] This is Symons' version of Mallarmé's: To name an object is to do away with three-quarters of the enjoyment of the poem.

[33] In fact, he expressed by implication the same idea much earlier in the poem "The Flame" (*P*, 50).

no impression, however carefully articulated, can, recorded, convey that feeling of sudden light which the works of art should and must convey."[34] And yet, Pound did not reject impressionism completely:

> Imagisme is not impressionism, *though one borrows,* or could borrow, *much from the impressionist method of presentation.*
>
> GB, 97

> The logical end of impressionist art is the *cinematograph.* The state of mind of the impressionist tends to become *cinematographical.*
>
> GB, 103

> One *does not* complain of neo-impressionism, or of accelerated impressionism and *"simultaneity,"* but one is not wholly satisfied by them.
>
> GB, 94
>
> (All italics mine)

As we shall see later, Pound's poetry contains many aspects that can only be understood in terms of "simultaneity" and "cinematography." Obviously, Pound was not opposed to the method of presentation, but he was not satisfied with the kind of impressionism represented by Symons (see "The Flame"), namely, the tendency toward superficial recording of impressions. He wanted to *select* impressions that would *dart inward* without discarding the sense of simultaneity in his presentation. Pound had noted that one remedy is symbolism. "In the 'eighties there were symbolists opposed to impressionists, now you have vorticism." (*GB,* 104) The fact that Pound put vorticism (imagism in poetry, cf. *GB,* 93) and symbolism in the same camp shows that both kinds of poetry, as distinct from impressionism, make every external object carry a subjective significance. Years earlier, Pound said, "The artist seeks out the luminous detail and presents it. He does not

[34] *Poetry Review,* 1 (March 1912), 133.

comment. His work remains the permanent basis of *psychology* and *metaphysics*."[35]

(Italics mine)

Pound also criticized the technique involved in symbolism, but his criticism seems to have included his own early poems (as well as his later poems which he did not foresee when he made the statement): "Imagisme is not symbolism. The symbolists dealt in 'association,' that is, in a sort of allusion." (*GB*, 97) The technique of "association" and "allusion" abounds in his early poetry, particularly in his Browningesque monologues.[36] His criticism of the symbol itself is more relevant to his poetry before 1914, and this criticism might have included Yeats: "The symbolist's symbols have a fixed value, like numbers in arithmetic, like 1, 2, and 7. The imagiste's images have a variable significance, like the signs a, b, and x in algebra." (*GB*, 97) He continued: "Almost anyone can realize that to use a symbol *with an ascribed or intended meaning is*, usually, to produce very bad art." (*GB*, 99) About a year before, Pound spoke unfavorably of Yeats: "Mr. Yeats has been subjective; believes in the glamour and associations which hang near the words. . . . He has much in common with the French symbolists. . . . Mr. Yeats' method is, to my way of thinking, very dangerous."[37] Around 1912 Yeats had not yet turned to symbols such as "blood," "gyre," and "tower" which could easily be considered symbols with an ascribed or intended meaning. However, there are still certain symbols in his early work that are subject to this charge. These are: the rose (of Rosicrucian and cabalistic doctrine), the tree (of life and knowledge), and the four elements of fire, earth, water, and air (wind). Unlike these, Pound asked that each image have a meaning definable only within the particular context in which it appears.

[35] *New Age*, x.6 (December 7, 1911), 130.

[36] The kind of "source-hunt" involved in most of these poems has led to at least two studies. See Nagy and Witemeyer.

[37] "Status Rerum," *Poetry*, 1.4 (January 1913), 125.

We can see now that although Pound asked practitioners to use symbols at face value— "a hawk is a hawk" (*LE*, 14), the image did not cease to be a hawk; it became a permanent metaphor for some subjective state or being. But the effort to turn an image into a permanent metaphor is, as Pound defined it, "symbolism" in its profounder sense. (*GB*, 97)

5

Between 1910 and 1913, Pound did place stronger emphasis upon "precision"; however, he had not eschewed the suggestive mode. Most of his poems written before 1914 reveal that he still indulged in the interplay of nuances of disjointed impressions and strove for the intensified metaphorical or "symbolic" function of the image.

It seems to me, therefore, that the movement of precision was directed exclusively against rhetoric (as distinguished from "method" of presentation). The revolt against rhetoric started with the poets of the 'nineties[38] who employed daily language in place of the choice diction and inversions of the Victorians.[39] Both Eliot and Pound acknowledged their debt to them. Eliot, in a tribute recorded for radio which celebrated the centenary of John Davidson's birth, says:

[38] *GB*, 98: "Whistler and Kandinsky and some cubists were set to getting extraneous matter out of their art; they were ousting literary values. The Flaubertians talk a good deal about 'constatation.' The 'nineties saw a movement against rhetoric. I think all these things move together, though they do not, of course, move in step."

See also "Verlaine" in Symons' *The Symbolist Movement in Literature*: " 'Take eloquence, and wring its neck!' said Verlaine in his 'Art Poétique'; and he showed, by writing it, that French verse could be written without rhetoric." Pp. 213-14.

[39] See, for instance, these few lines in A. Beardsley's *The Three Musicians*:

> The tourist gives a furious glance
> Red as his guide-book grows, moves on, and offers up
> a prayer for France.

Notice the modern diction *tourist* and *guide-book* and the conversational tone.

. . . I was reading the poets of the 'nineties, who were the only poets . . . who at that period of history seemed to have anything to offer to me as a beginner. What I wanted, I think, from the poets of the 'nineties was what they did not have in common with the Pre-Raphaelites, but what was new and original in their work. And I remember three poets in particular. One was Arthur Symons, some of his poems; another was Ernest Dowson, again one or two poems; and the third was Davidson. . . . From these men I got the idea that one could write poetry in an English such as one would speak oneself. A colloquial idiom. There was spoken rhythm in some of their poems.[40]

Pound admitted many times in his *Letters* his debt to the poets of the 'nineties, but his earliest public testimony is found in his Preface to *The Poetical Works of Lionel Johnson* (London, 1915): "In America ten or twelve years ago one read Fiona MacLeod, and Dowson, and Symons. . . . One is drunk . . . with Dowson's 'Cynara,' and with one or two poems of Symons' 'Wanderers'." (*LE*, 367) Symons' "Wanderers" prefigured the conversational opening of Pound's poem "Cino."[41]

But the crisis in the development of Pound's language (diction and structure) did not come until he was spurred by Ford Madox Hueffer's idea of modernity. Recent scholarship has revealed that Hueffer (later named Ford), rather than Hulme, was, by and large, the dominant influence on Pound in this respect.[42]

[40] Quoted in Maurice Lindsay's "Introduction" to *John Davidson: A Selection of his Poems* (London, 1961), pp. 8-9.

[41] See Witemeyer, p. 131. Compare Symons' lines, "I have had enough of women, and enough of love" with the opening lines of "Cino," "Bah! I have sung women in three cities,/ But it is all the same;/ And I will sing of the sun." Cf. also Symons' translation of Verlaine's "Les Indolents" which begins with "Bah! spite of Fate."

[42] See Noel Stock, *Poet in Exile* (New York, 1964), pp. 45-48; Schneidau, Chapter v; Witemeyer, Appendix B.

Pound had been with the Hulme group in the Soho restaurants since 1909, but Pound was still preoccupied with medieval subjects and was continuously experimenting with medieval rhythms. He was still writing "shady" poems in a somewhat outdated diction and with many inversions:

> Heart mine, art mine, whose embraces
> Clasp but wind that past thee bloweth?
> E'en this air so subtly gloweth,
> Guerdoned by thy son-gold traces,
> That my heart is half-afraid
> For the fragrance on him laid;
> Even so love's might amazes!

According to Pound, when he showed his *Canzoni* (1911) (from which the above is taken) to Ford Madox Hueffer in Germany, Hueffer (who had earlier published his aim: "to register my own times in terms of my own time")[43] felt so uncomfortable about Pound's medievalism and archaism that he rolled on the floor to show how dislocated his style was from his time. "And that roll," Pound continues, "saved me at least two years, perhaps more. It sent me back to my own proper effort, namely, toward using the living tongue."[44]

And sometime after that year, we begin to see in Pound a drastic change in diction and line structure. We know that one poem scheduled to appear in the *Canzoni* was "Redondillas, or Something of that Sort," but it was withdrawn from the printer. This poem, as we look at it now, was indeed out of key with the rest of Pound's early poems, and, in particular, with the poems in *Canzoni*. Had this poem been included, Ford Madox Hueffer might have hesitated to attack Pound as an out-and-out medievalist, although he might not have

---

[43] Preface to *Collected Poems*, 1911.

[44] Obituary Notice on Ford (August 1939 issue of *Nineteenth Century and After CXXVI*, p. 179). This event has been well pursued by Noel Stock, Schneidau, and Witemeyer. See note 42.

liked the poem either. "Redondillas" is pronounced Whitman-
ism:

> I sing the gaudy to-day and cosmopolite civilization
> Of my hatred of crudities, of weariness of banalities.
> I sing of the ways that I love, of Beauty and delicate
> savours
>
> . . . .
>
> I would sing the American people, God send them
> some civilization. . . .[45]

Yet one year later Pound included in *The Ripostes* (1912)
"The Alchemist." Although this poem is much more con-
centrated in line structure and subtler in music than "Redondillas," it contains aspects of the Whitmanesque style:

> From the plum-colored lake, in stillness,
> From the molten dyes of the water
> Bring the burnished nature of fire;
> Briseis, Lianor, Loica,
> From the white earth and the olive
> From the poplars weeping their amber,
>
> . . . .
>
> From the power of grass,
> From the white, alive in the seed,
> From the heat of the bud,
> From the copper of the leaf in autumn.

P, 75-76

More poems of this style appear in *Lustra* (1914, written 1913)
as, for example, "Salutation" (*P*, 85), "Commission" (*P*, 88),
"Further Instructions" (*P*, 94) as well as the undeniably Whitmanesque "Pax Saturni" (*Poetry* II [April 1913], 8-10) and
"The Choice" (*Poetry* III [November 1913], 54).

[45] This poem was reprinted recently by Grace Perry in *Poetry
Australia*, No. 15 (Sidney, Australia, April 1967), 5-11. These lines are
quoted by permission of Dr. Perry.

In most of the poems in the *Ripostes*, the employment of modern diction is already obvious. Except for some "thee's," "thy's," and abbreviations like " 'neath" " 'mid," we do not find many inversions nor obsessively archaic diction. ("The Seafarer" is an exception, being an attempt to preserve the flavor of the Anglo-Saxon). The language in "A Girl" needs almost no change to read like a poem written in today's English.

> The tree has entered my hands,
> The sap has ascended my arms,
> The tree has grown in my breast—
> Downward,
> The branches grow out of me, like arms,
>
> Tree you are,
> Moss you are,
> You are violets with wind above them,
> A child—*so* high—you are
> And all this is folly to the world.

P, 62

When the next groups of poems appeared in *Poetry* (April 1913 and November 1913) and in the *New Freewoman* (December 1913), all "thou's" and "thee's" (except one or two cases in which distinctive ancient "feeling" is involved) and abbreviations disappeared. Instead we have an unruffled and uninvolved syntax.

This tendency reveals one fact: as Pound moved toward 1914 (at about which time he actually started translating Chinese poems from the Fenollosa notebooks), he was obsessed with the effort to use no involved syntax, no archaic diction, and no inversions. The language in *Cathay* is comparatively more relevant to Pound's modernism than most of his other translations, because it is a continuation of this tendency.

His other translations were made from Romance or Germanic languages. Closely related to these languages, the English vocabulary often suggests direct equivalents (sometimes in obsolete forms). Translators from these languages, like Pound, are tempted to preserve the flavor and the full suggestiveness of a certain word in the original by using a rare word in English at the expense of its obsoleteness. Most of Pound's translations prior to *Cathay* retain an easily recognizable stamp of the original, in form, syntax, and diction. This is most obvious in his translation of "The Seafarer." In a sense, Pound's feeling for identification seemed so strong that he could hardly release himself completely from the fetters of the linguistic lineage. Instead of "tell" for "wrecan," he used "reckon," a more dated word, because "reckon" sounded like "wrecan" and yet carried the meaning of "tell." One can spot many such "rarities" in Pound's medieval and Provençal translations, but not in *Cathay*. With no linguistic connection to suggest verbal equivalents, Pound was free to pick the most contemporary diction without feeling unjust to the original. In a sense, this gave him a sudden liberation from the linguistic bondage he had imposed upon himself all these years. And yet, had Pound come upon these notebooks four years earlier when he was locked between archaism and inversions, he might not have produced these poems in a language that evoked such high praise from Ford Madox Hueffer: "If these are original verses, then Mr. Pound is the greatest poet of this day. . . . The poems in *Cathay* are things of a supreme beauty. What poetry should be, that they are."[46]

But the stress upon Whitmanesque progression and unruffled syntax should not lead us away from Pound's basic obsession with indirect presentation. The first imagist rule: "Direct treatment of the thing whether subjective or objective," is but a general statement of their stylistic direction.

[46] Quoted in Eliot's *Ezra Pound: His Metric and Poetry* (1917), reprinted in *To Criticize the Critic* (London, 1965), pp. 180-81.

Pound's image is one "which presents an *intellectual* and *emotional complex* in an instant of time." (March 1913, *LE*, 4) The emphasis is upon the *speed* ("in an instant of time") of the transference of the signification of the image which is complex both *intellectually* and *emotionally*. This is basically at variance with most instinctive poetry. Instead of bursting into images and sounds arbitrarily, Pound *selects* and *arranges* his images and sounds. The process of selection makes him a conscious and sophisticated artist, not a spontaneous nightingale. If his later *Cantos* appear to be spontaneous through quick shifts in free association, it is a calculated spontaneity through the manipulation of the surface.

In the more important poems in the two volumes prior to *Cathay*, we find two artistic processes. One is the process of intensification. Pound's description of turning a thirty-line poem into a two-line poem ("In a Station of the Metro") through "a second intensity" is a well-known paradigm of his mind at work. (*GB*, 103) Just what exactly was the previous form of this poem we do not know, but Pound gave us a hint. In "How I Began" in *T. P.'s Weekly* (June 6, 1963, 707) Pound mentioned an early poem, "Piccadilly," another poem of the *face motif*, in connection with his composition of "In a Station of the Metro": "I waited three years to find the words for 'Piccadilly,' it is eight lines long, and they tell me now it is 'sentiment.' For well over a year I have been trying to make a poem of a very beautiful thing that befell me in the Paris underground. I got out of a train at, I think, La Concorde and in the jostle I saw a beautiful face, and then, turning suddenly, another and another, and then a beautiful child's face, and then another beautiful face." "Piccadilly" was written in 1909, but it is strange that it should begin with "Beautiful, tragical faces. . . ." The previous form of "In a Station of the Metro" must be different from "Piccadilly," we assume. But why should Pound mention it in this connection? Why did he finally omit it from his later editions

58

of the *Personae?* Quite possibly, as far as the method of presentation is concerned, the previous form of "In a Station of the Metro" showed no improvement upon "Piccadilly." It is, therefore, worthwhile to compare these two poems to see how one, through intensification, actually gives us more than the other, longer poem.

Piccadilly

Beautiful, tragical faces,
Ye that were whole, and are so sunken;
And, O ye vile, ye that might have been loved,
That are so sodden and drunken,
      Who hath forgotten you?

O wistful, fragile faces, few out of many!

The gross, the coarse, the brazen,
God knows I cannot pity them, perhaps, as I should do,
But, oh, ye delicate, wistful faces
      Who hath forgotten you?[47]

In a Station of the Metro

The apparition of these faces in the crowd;
Petals on a wet, black bough.

P, 109

"Piccadilly" reads flat because of the overt way in which the description of these faces is given. The pathos derives from an *obvious* contrast and irony—"beautiful" but "tragical." The rest is a logical elaboration on this contrast: "whole" (in the past), but "sunken" (now), "that might have been loved," but "sodden and drunken" (now). There is nothing intricate about the process of interiorization of the face image. Worst of all, the wretched state of these faces is drawn in logical terms: *were* and *are* easily indicate the vicissitude of time.

[47] *Personae* (London, 1909), p. 56.

But not so with "In a Station of the Metro." All the attributes of the faces ("beautiful" etc.) are suppressed. What is left is the uncertain, shady, strongly emotional, ethereal and incorporal quality of the moment in the word "apparition," a word that calls forth not one definite shade of meaning, but several levels of suggestiveness. It does not say whether the faces are beautiful, fearful, sunken, tragical, but it suggests them all. And the gist of the moment so captured is juxtaposed with a natural scene. The strong identification of the faces with the petals on a wet, black bough is enforced by the selected epithet of "emotional apparition" *black*, a quality that corresponds with, and merges into, the word *apparition*. This is why Pound described the poem as follows: "a thing outward and objective transforms itself, or darts into a thing inward and subjective." (*GB*, 103)

Similar intensification is found in "The Fan Piece, for her Imperial Lord." Working from one of Giles' translations of a Chinese poem of ten lines, he intensified it into three short lines:

GILES

O fair white silk, fresh from the weaver's loom,
Clear as the frost, bright as the winter snow—
See! friendship fashions out of thee a fan,
Round as the round moon shines in heaven's above,
At home, abroad, a close companion thou,
Stirring at every move the grateful gale.
And yet I fear, ah me! that autumn chills,
Cooling the dying summer's torrid rage,
Will see thee laid neglected on the shelf,
All thoughts of bygone days, like them bygone.[48]

[48] Giles, *A History of Chinese Literature* (New York, 1901), p. 101. The discussion of this poem in relation to the original is not relevant here, because at this point, Pound did not know the original poem. cf. *Spectrum*, 26.

POUND
> O fan of white silk,
>   clear as frost on the grass-blade.
> You also are laid aside.

                                    P, 108

In Giles, a human situation—the vicissitude of time causing
the neglect of the lady—is compared to a fan. The merits of
this lady are given in terms of the attributes of the fan, laid
out in flat epithets: *fair, fresh, clear, bright, round* (meaning
full, complete, whole). The change of her state is clearly
narrated (or stated). Pound retains only two striking features
without humanized meaning, *whiteness* and *clearness* and
splashes these on a new background, *a grass-blade*, giving still
greater prominence to the two features of the fan. This object,
so seen, is turned metaphorically into a human situation. The
obvious comparisons in Giles' version are suppressed and their
relation is retained only barely by the word *also*. If it were an
original poem by Pound, he might have dropped the word
also to let one plane of experience cut into another, as he did
in the Metro piece and some other poems.

   But this is enough to show how much Pound was dissatisfied with direct description and how much Pound, as in the
case of the Metro piece, tried to avoid the logic of obvious
sequential relation and preferred a "leap" in logic. This is the
second aspect of Pound's indirection. This leap of logic, as we
can see now, is clearly a product of both impressionism and
symbolism: both are marked by the absence of links of connection and result in disconnected phases of perception and
a sense of simultaneity. The Metro piece is, in many ways, an
impressionist poem. When the poem was first published in
Poetry II.1 (April 1913), it was laid out graphically in the
following manner:

The apparition   of these faces   in the crowd :
Petals   on a wet, black   bough. (p. 12)[49]

Pound's intention to arrange the poem into phases of perception is too obvious to need explanation. But even taking the later printed form, we can still see that it consists of two unconnected (syntactically speaking) impressions: that of the faces and that of the petals. But at the same time it is not an impressionist poem, because the two impressions do not stop at being superficial impressions. They turn inward, first, through what we might call emotional correspondence ("black" calls up "apparition") and second through the withdrawal of the key of connections between the two impressions, giving them a simultaneous flash upon the reader's screen of imagination, forcing the two impressions to overlie and to inter-define each other.

This sophisticated indirection and suggestiveness in the midst of clear, striking images marked Pound off from most other imagist poets. This is also why I think it misleading to say that this poem is the best exponent of T. E. Hulme's kind of imagist poem, as Howard J. Waskow tries to show in his *Whitman: Explorations in Form* (London, 1966), p. 111. His supporting statement is from Hulme's "A Lecture on Modern Poetry": "Say the poet is moved by a certain landscape, he selects from that certain images which, put into juxtaposition in separate lines, serve to suggest and evoke the state he feels. . . . Two visual images form what one may call a visual chord. They unite to suggest an image which is different to both." This statement indeed explains one aspect of Pound's method

---

[49] Hugh Kenner in "The Invention of China" also points out this graphic layout in relation to the Chinese language. This layout must have been something of significance to Pound, for Richard Aldington did not forget to imitate this arrangement in his parodies of *Lustra*:

    The apparition   of these poems   in a crowd:
    White faces   in a black   dead faint.

                The Egoist, 1 (July 15, 1914), p. 273.

of presentation, namely the surface interplay of visual images. But T. E. Hulme's own poems never displayed the kind of sophisticated process of internalization that most of Pound's poems have.

In Hulme, a hawk is a hawk, a moon is a moon. His subtlety consists of two types. (1) A resemblance (rarely unstated) between two *visual* objects which seldom turn inward. But Pound is never content with merely visual images. A counterpart from human situations, emotionally charged and intensified, is always there, although it may be unstated. The image of a moon tangled in the tall mast resembling a child's balloon forgotten after play in Hulme's "Above the Dock" will reveal, under Pound's hand, some "fearful," or "tense" feeling. And Pound would never make such sloppy statements as "*What seems so far away is but* a child's balloon." Pound would speed it up by eliminating most of these words. "A touch of cold in the autumn night" (in "Autumn") would probably be rewritten with the word "touch" changed into a word of multiple suggestive force. (2) Hulme likes to insert a pretentious impenetrability of some subjective truth that is absent, "I do not stop to speak, but nodded." This is nothing but rhetoric. At best, it is but a *topoi* of excuse for some inexpressibility, a verbal trick. Pound seldom has such pretentious rhetoric. The subterranean transference of two external scenes, one human, one natural (in the Metro piece), into a subjective state within the scenes by dint of what Pound once called the "language beyond metaphor" is something Hulme never aspires to.

With this understanding of the legacy Pound inherited from impressionism and symbolism, of his stress upon clear images in neat modern diction, and upon a sophisticated process of internalization, we can no longer call him a pure precisionist. His obsession with suggestion as a potential poetic expression explains not only a poem like "The Return," but also the changes he makes in a poem such as "Liu Ch'e," which he reworked from Giles' version of a Chinese poem.

GILES

The sound of rustling silk is stilled,
With dust the marble courtyard filled;
No footfalls echo on the floor,
Fallen leaves in heaps block up the door . . .
For she, my pride, my lovely one is lost
And I am left, in hopeless anguish tossed.[50]

POUND

The rustling of the silk is discontinued,
Dust drifts over the courtyard,
There is no sound of footfall, and the leaves
Scurry into heaps and lie still,
And she the rejoicer of the heart is beneath them:

A wet leaf that clings to the threshold.

P, 108

Here is an example of improvement not in rhetoric and rhythm alone (Pound's is, of course, *vers libre*), but also on the level of suggestion. The first four lines are made up of four self-contained images. A self-contained image is one that carries such poetic feeling or idea that it can sometimes stand alone as a poem. Each image here represents, in its own way, the loss or absence of a lovely thing. I think, except for stylistic superiority, both versions succeed in getting across this general effect made up by the first four lines. The difference lies, of course, in the change Pound makes in the last line. Instead of an open statement of the result of this loss ("And I am left, in hopeless anguish tossed"), Pound suppresses this direct venting of grief and employs an image that strongly suggests it.[51]

[50] Giles, p. 100.
[51] Contrary to this is the poem "Ione, Dead the Long Year" in which the statement of the absence of Ione is direct: "Empty are the ways

64

But what does "a wet leaf that clings to the threshold" (which is Pound's sheer invention) represent? Indeed, within the context built up thus far, it has to represent some kind of profound grief, but the image does not stop at being just that; it embraces more.

It needs little thinking to understand the symbolic meaning of "leaf that clings to the threshold"—*leaf*, now fallen, representing death, *clings* showing the emotional attachment that goes on after death. But what about *wet*? It is no coincidence that this line should remind us of other similar lines in Pound's imagist poems. Compare the structure and diction of this line to

Petals on a *wet*, black bough.

The petals fall in the fountain,
The orange-coloured rose-leaves,
Their ochre *clings* to the stone.
                                        "Ts'ai Chi'h," *P*, 108

As cool as the pale *wet* leaves of lily-of-the-valley
She lay beside me in the dawn.[52]
                                        "Alba," *P*, 109

The *dew* is upon the *leaf*
The night about us is restless.
                                        "Coitus," *P*, 110
                                        (All italics mine)

It seems to me that Pound, even as late as 1913, still liked to attach to certain adjectives a general emotional symbolism. We have seen him use the word "white" in "The White Stag" (1908) and "black" in the Metro piece, which is, like Yeats' "black wind," transensuous and suggestive. The word "wet" in these lines seems to belong to this category—suggesting

of this land/ Where Ione/ Walked once, and now does not walk/ But seems like a person just gone." (*P*, 112)
[52] Compare this poem to the structure of "Fan-Piece."

65

perhaps a distressing, dismal, beaten emotion(?). But adjectives of this kind promise no definite meaning; several shades of emotional significance seem to have clustered around them, although they seem also to strike instantly on the chord of our sensibility.

6

Let us return to the beginning of this chapter and try to understand Pound's fervor for the poem "The Jewel Stairs' Grievance:"

jade	step(s)	grow	white	dew(s)
night	late	attack(soak)	gauze	stocking(s)
let	down	crystal		blind
glass-clear		watch	autumn	moon[53]

Pound's version:

The jewelled steps are already quite white with dew,
It is so late that the dew soaks my gauze stockings,
And I let down the crystal curtain
And watch the moon through the clear autumn.

NOTE: Jewel stairs, therefore a palace. Grievance, therefore there is something to complain of. Gauze stockings, therefore, a court lady, not a servant who complains. Clear autumn, therefore he has no excuse on account of weather. Also she has come early, for the dew has not merely whitened the stairs, but has soaked her stockings. The poem is especially prized because she utters *no direct reproach.*   (Italics mine)

Ideally, of course, the poem should be understood in terms of the "genre" after which Li Po modeled it.[54] But Pound did

---

[53] Again we do not have this example from Fenollosa's notebook. This is a word-for-word annotation of the poem.

[54] As, for instance, Hsieh T'iao's (464-499) poem of the same title: "I let down the beaded blind in the hall at night./ Fireflies fly around

not have the knowledge of Chinese to do this, nor (it seems) did Fenollosa do much of that kind of research. The point that concerns us here is that Pound valued this poem for its "indirection," for the process in which the images point, or take the reader back, to the original situation in order to sense out the kind of grief imbued in this scene—thus turning the clear, but external images inward, weaving them into a tragic human state. Ezra Pound, as we remember, had not been satisfied with the obtruding function of the symbols (*LE*, 14: "If a man use 'symbols,' he must use them so that their symbolic function does not obtrude"), although, up to this point, we still find traces of symbolic devices in his work that are at variance with his advocacy of the natural object as an *adequate* symbol. The kind of indirection in "The Jewel Stairs' Grievance" does not involve, strictly speaking, any sort of symbolic function, for we can hardly say what particular idea the images stand for. They almost fulfill what Pound implies in the phrase "a hawk is a hawk." And yet, through selected details, through these objective and external "impressions," the poem has arrested an atmosphere that *evokes* (but *does not state*) the tragic human situation looming far behind these surface manifestations.

This method of selected details (see Chapter I) that are free from overt and contrived subjectification is even clearer in the original in which the absence of the personal pronoun (protagonist in the situation) immediately universalizes the situation. This absence, aided by the syntactical peculiarities (verbs without declension and tense), has, in a strange way, turned these surface manifestations impressionistic, for the poem actually reads, in perhaps awkward English, like this:

Jade steps grow white dew(s)
Night late (:) soak gauze stocking(s)

and take rest./ Through the long night I sew gauze dresses./ How can there be an end to my thoughts of you?"

Let(s) down the crystal blind

(To) see, glass-clear, the autumn moon

We know that most Chinese poems from Fenollosa's notebooks are often provided first with word-for-word English
equivalents and a prose crib.[55] One can imagine that Pound,
reading these, would sense the similarity of disconnectedness
in style (from the viewpoint of English grammar) to impressionism. Pound made many such approximations in the
Cantos. (See Chapter I and concluding lines in Chapter IV).

The absence of the protagonist will stir up (at least in an
English reader) these questions: Who lets down the blind
and watches the autumn moon? The traditional motif enables us to know this is a court-lady (as the details support
it), but one specific lady or all other ladies of the same fate?
The answer is, of course, both. But because the linguistic
peculiarities have made it possible not to restrict the situation
to one participant, the reader's presence (with the protagonist)
in the midst of the surface manifestations is invited. It is as if
all these occur dramatically right before his eyes—time and
space becoming meaningless. Pound's interest in this poem
seemed to hover between the directness of impressions and
indirect evocation of a tragic human state, for until he dealt
with the *Cathay* poems, he had been trying to arrest, in clear
images, such an inward-moving instant. (*GB*, 103)

Before we attempt to see how Pound's own practice conditioned his other translations in the next two chapters, it is
perhaps relevant to ask here why he did not try to avoid
using the personal pronoun in rendering this poem. The answer is that he was obsessed with uninvolved syntax. It could
be expected that he would not use more elliptical expressions,
such as

[55] See Appendix I and Kenner, "Ezra Pound and Chinese," *Agenda*,
IV (October-November 1965), 38-41.

Orion at sunrise.
Horses now with black manes.
Eat dog meat.
Canto, 64/101

Prayer: hands uplifted
Solitude: a person, a NURSE
Canto, 52/6

to get rid of the commitment of the personal pronoun.[56] This
is also why he did not translate "Floating clouds (:) (a)
wanderer's thought" (see Chapter I) into a line of this kind
of structure:

Moon on the palm-leaf,
confusion
Canto, 21/100

These revolutionary techniques came later. But even in these
transforming years, Pound had already tried to achieve this
kind of elliptical effect by the peculiar manipulation of the
line unit which we shall see in Chapter IV.

[56] As to whether it is better to use "she" instead of "I" in "The
Jewel Stairs' Grievance," it is a matter of personal preference and
interpretation. I think each has its own validity—if a pronoun is
unavoidable in this case.

chapter three

His "Maestria" in Translation:
Limitations and Breakthrough

1

I resolved . . . that I would know the dynamic content from the shell, that I would know what was accounted poetry everywhere, what part of poetry was "indestructible," what part could *not be lost* by translation, and—scarcely less important—what effects were obtainable in *one* language only and were utterly incapable of being translated.

"How I Began," in *T. P.'s Weekly*
(June 6, 1913), 707.

POUND makes it very clear in this passage that total translation is impossible. He aims at the transmission of the "indestructible" part of the poem and lets the rest go. *Effect* is the goal toward which the translator should strive. It is no accident that in the same essay Pound should also be talking about the process of getting a calculated effect in his poem "In a Station of the Metro." (Cf. Chapter II) In translation, too, he aims at finding "equations for the human emotions," (*SR*, 5) and to be able to achieve this, he must be able to distinguish the "dynamic content from the shell." This basic position of Pound's remained unchanged throughout his early years until at least 1918. He reaffirmed this position in his study of French poets:

. . . certain things are translatable from one language to another, a tale or an image will "translate," music will, practi-

70

cally never, translate; and if a work be taken abroad in the original tongue, certain properties seem to become less apparent, or less important. Fancy styles, questions of local "taste," lose importance. Even though I know the overwhelming importance of technique, technicalities in a foreign tongue cannot have for me the importance they have to a man writing in that tongue; almost the only technique perceptible to a foreigner is the presentation of content as free as possible from the clutteration of dead technicalities, fustian à la Louis XV; and from timidities of workmanship. This is perhaps the only technique that ever matters, the only *maestria*.[1]

The idea that "an image will 'translate' and music will, practically never, translate" was implied in "A Few Don'ts" (1912, *LE*, 7) and extended in "How To Read" (1928, *LE*, 25) in the triple concept of *melopoeia* (the "musical property" that directs the bearing or trend of the meaning of the words), *phanopoeia* ("a casting of images upon the visual imagination") and *logopoeia* ("the dance of the intellect among words"):

It is practically impossible to transfer or translate it [i.e. *melopoeia*] from one language to another, save perhaps by divine accident, and for half a line at a time.

Phanopoeia can, on the other hand, be translated almost, or wholly, intact. . . .

Logopoeia does not translate; though the attitude of mind may pass through a paraphrase. Or one might say, you can *not* translate it "locally," but having determined the original author's state of mind, you may or may not be able to find a derivative or an equivalent.

A number of questions are apt to arise: What is the relation of *logopoeia* to "the presentation of content" or to "the dynamic

[1] "French Poets," *Little Review*, iv.10 (February 1918), [3]-61. *MIN*, 159-60.

content" quoted above? The core or "indestructible" part of the poem, according to Pound, is the "state of mind" of the original author as it is determined by the translator. How and to what extent can this be done? In other words, what exactly does Pound mean by "content"? why "dynamic"? Elsewhere, Pound talks about setting forth the *meaning* as the best service he can render the audience in his translation of Guido Cavalcanti.[2] Does the word "content" mean the same as the "prose-sense" of the poem? In his "Translators of Greek" (August 1918), Pound praises Hugh Salel, Gavin Douglas, and Arthur Golding as superb and delightful translators for their absorption in *subject-matter*: "Salel is a most delightful approach to the Iliads; he is still absorbed in the subject-matter, as Douglas and Golding were absorbed in their subject-matter." (*LE*, 254; *MIN*, 132) Does "content" mean "subject-matter?"

The problem is that the contours of these three terms—content, subject-matter, and meaning—are not as distinct as they promise to be. This is at least true of Pound's use of them. The inherent ambiguity of these words is best demonstrated by the fact that I. A. Richards had to write a whole book to define *The Meaning of Meaning*. When Pound employs the word "content," or "meaning," does he have in mind the paraphrasable meaning (i.e. a message or moral or thought or belief) for which the words are but a vehicle? Or is he thinking about an inexpressible state of being or emotion which is to be sought, in T. S. Eliot's words, "beyond poetry,"[3] the thing attainable only through hints and not through statements? Or is he already with the New Critics who insist

[2] Letter to *TLS* (December 6, 1912) in answer to the reviewer of his translations from Guido Cavalcanti.

[3] "In reading [poetry] we are intent on what the poem *points at*, and not on the poetry, this seems to me the thing to try for. To get *beyond poetry* as Beethoven in his later works, strove to get *beyond music*." From an unpublished lecture quoted in *The Achievement of T. S. Eliot* by F. O. Matthiessen (Oxford, 1948), p. 90.

72

upon the so-called representational meaning which is to be established *within* and *among* the words themselves and consider all references to the outside world as nonaesthetic?[4]

It has been made abundantly clear by many critics that Pound renounced "didacticism" as early as 1908. (See Chapter II),[5] and so we can be quite sure that by "the presentation of content" Pound does not mean the presentation of the propositions of the poem. In fact, Pound has been even more specific: " 'Thought' as Browning understood it—'ideas' as the term is current, are poor two-dimensional stuff, a scant, scratch covering. 'Damn ideas, anyhow.' An idea is only an imperfect induction of fact." (*MIN*, 147; *LE*, 267) Pound has gone even further. Attacking the scholars' philological concern in their reading of the classics, he rejects the word-sense and phrase-sense as the entrance to the poem. What is important is for the translator to grasp the thing. Parallel to his theory of "absolute rhythm" (1910, 1912) and to his theory of "absolute metaphor" (1910, 1914),[6] we seem to have what might

[4] Here I am following chiefly M. Krieger's classification in his contributing article to Preminger's *Encyclopedia of Poetry and Poetics* (Princeton, 1965), pp. 475-79. Without knowing this article, I had written an essay on the same problem focusing my discussion on the various criticisms of one Chinese poem throughout the centuries entitled *Several Approaches to T'ao Ch'ien's Drinking Song V: the Problem of Meaning*. Since Mr. Krieger's article is more relevant in relation to the development of English poetry and criticism, I find it best to use his classification here.

[5] This refers to Pound's earliest testimony in his letter to William Carlos Williams:

    1. To paint the thing as I see it.

    2. Beauty.

    3. Freedom from didacticism.—(*Letters*, 6).

[6] "As for the verse itself: I believe in an ultimate and absolute rhythm as I believe in an absolute symbol or metaphor." "Introduction" to Cavalcanti Poems (November 15, 1910), *Translations*, p. 23. "I believe in an 'absolute rhythm' . . ." "Prolegomena" (February 1912), also in *LE* p. 9. "I said in the preface to my *Guido Cavalcanti* that I believe in absolute rhythm. . . . To hold a like belief, in a sort of permanent metaphor is, as I understand it, 'symbolism' in its profounder sense." *GB*, 97.

be called the "absolute poem," the Platonic form of the poem. Instead of the "thought" of the poem, Pound gives us "the internal thought-form." (In the case of rhythm Pound has offered what he called "the inner form of the line" which may be considered an alternate term for "absolute rhythm.")[7] Discussing Arnaut's "En Breu Brisaral Temps Braus," he says, "Beyond its external symmetry [rhyming schemes etc.], the formal poem should have its internal thought-form, or at least, thought progress. This form can, of course, be as well displayed in a prose version as in a metrical one."[8] He then offers us his prose version of this poem which he later re-translated into metrical form. The difference in form and texture between the two versions is obvious. Let us quote the first stanza from both versions:

> Soon will the harsh time break upon us, the north wind hoot in the branches which all swish together with their closed-over boughs of leaves; no bird sings nor "peeps" now, yet love teaches me to make a song that shall not be second nor third, but first for freeing the embittered heart.
>
> *New Age*, x.16 (February 15, 1912), 369.

> Briefly bursteth season brisk,
> Blasty north breeze racketh branch,
> Branches rasp each branch on each
> Tearing twig and tearing leafage,
>   Chirms now no bird nor cries querulous;
> So Love demands I make outright
> A song that no song shall surpass
>   For freeing the heart of sorrow.
>
> 1920, *Translations*, 169.

Similarly, part of Arnaut's "L'Aura Amara" which has a

---

[7] "I gather the Limbs of Osiris," *New Age*, x. 15 (February 8, 1912), 344.
[8] *Ibid.*, *New Age*, x.16 (February 15, 1912), 369.

highy complex metrical arrangement had been rendered by Pound simultaneously into three versions: first, an equivalent in English meters; second, a prose version; and third, an approximation in keeping with the original rhyming scheme. (The fourth in *Instigations* is an improvement on the third.) Of the third, which most resembles the original, he said: "The choppy lines do not affect the rhythm for reading, directly or necessarily; the poems in the old manuscript are written straight along like prose. I print the verses in this form only better to indicate the rhyme scheme."[9]

Pound seemed to believe that none of these forms he adopted had significantly affected the poem *itself*, or what he liked to call "the beauty of the *thing*." Once the poet dwells in the *thing*, his poetry will be freed from the dangers of rhetoric and prolixity and become alive:

For it is not until poetry lives again "close to the thing" that it will be a vital part of contemporary life.

The only way to escape from rhetoric and frilled paper decoration is through beauty—"beauty of the thing."

I have no especial interest in rhyme. It tends to draw away the artist's attention from forty to ninety per cent of his syllables and concentrate it on the admittedly more prominent reminder. It tends to draw him into prolixity and pull him away from the thing.[10]

As a translator, Browning was inferior to Rossetti not because of rhetoric, but because of his failure to concentrate on the thing: ". . . obscurities due not to the thing but to the wording, are a botch, and are not worth preserving in a translation. . . . Rossetti is in this matter sounder than Browning, when he says that the only thing worth bringing over is the

[9] "I Gather the Limbs of Osiris," *New Age*, x.11 (January 11, 1912), 250.
[10] All from "I Gather the Limbs of Osiris," *New Age*, x.16 (February 15, 1912), 370.

beauty of the original; and despite Rossetti's purple plush and molasses trimmings he meant by 'beauty' something fairly near what we mean by the 'emotional intensity' of his original." (*MIN*, 149; *LE*, 268)

One thing at least is clear: Pound never aims at becoming what Jean Paris calls "a rationalist translator" who "is satisfied when he has expressed what he believes to be 'the ideas of the author' with a minimum of misinterpretations."[11]

But what does Pound mean by "emotional intensity?" Naturally, one recalls Pound's early statement that poetry is "equations for emotions." Does Pound simply think, then, that "content" means "emotions?" Here the intrigue comes in. For there is a distinction between the emotion before it enters the poem and the emotion that has transformed itself, grown and changed with the words in the poem. One is emotion, the raw material, so to speak, and the other is the aesthetic experience inhering in and coming out of the artistic process of intensification of *that* emotion.

As we now see, Pound meaningfully adds the word "dynamic" before the word "content." It is the artistic "life" of that emotion, the experiencing of that emotion *in* the poem that counts. It also dawns upon us that there is a special significance in the fact that Pound stated and re-stated throughout these years the concept of *energy* in poetry. The duty of the translator is to transport this "dynamic content," the lifeforce of the poem, to the reader. Let us look at some critical statements by Pound to see how this concept of energy has surged in his mind:

The spirit of the arts is *dynamic*.

1910, *SR*, 234.

[11] Jean Paris, "Translation and Creation" in *The Craft and Context of Translation: A Critical Symposium*, eds., William Arrowsmith and Roger Shattuck (Austin, Texas, 1961), p. 57.

Rodin's belief that *energy* is beauty holds thus far, namely, that all our ideas of beauty of line are in some way connected with our idea of *swiftness* or easy power of *motion*.

1910, "Introduction" to Cavalcanti Poems, *Translations*, 23.

In every art I can think of we are damned and clogged by the mimetic; *dynamic* acting is nearly forgotten.

"I Gather the Limbs of Osiris," *New Age*, x.16 (February 15, 1912), 370.

We might come to believe that the thing that matters in art is a sort of *energy*, something more or less like electricity or radio-activity, a *force* transfusing, welding and unifying.

1912, "The Serious Artist" in *LE*, 49.

I believe that poetry is the more highly *energized*.

1912, *LE*, 49.

Poetry is a centaur. The thinking word-arranging, clarifying faculty must *move* and *leap* with the *energizing*, sentient, musical faculties.

1912, *LE*, 52.

Aristotle will tell you that 'The apt use of metaphor, being as it is, the swift perception of relations, is the true hallmark of genius . . .' by 'apt use,' I should say it were well to understand, a *swiftness*, almost a *violence*.

1912, *LE*, 52.

I defined the vortex as *"the point of maximum energy."*

1914, *GB*, 93.

(All italics mine)

The "indestructible" part or core of the poem is to be sought in the emotion *energized* in and by the words, not the emotion before it enters the poem. It is "the solid, the 'last atom of force verging off into the first atom of matter.'" (1918, *MIN.* 147)

The translator must find his transmittible equivalent in the energy and force of emotion residing in the words; how he is to achieve this remains to be defined. Pound has provided us with what he has called "Technique of Content" (1912):

Let us imagine that words are like great hollow cones of steel of different dullness and acuteness; I say great because I want them not too easy to move; they must be of different sizes. Let us imagine them charged with a force like electricity, or, rather, radiating a force from their apexes—some radiating, some sucking in. We must have a greater variety of activity than with electricity—not merely positive and negative; but let us say $+$, $-$, $\times$, $+$, ^{+}a, $-a$, $\times a$, $+a$, etc. Some of these kinds of forces neutralize each other, some augment; but the only way any two cones can be got to act without waste is for them to be so placed that their apexes and a line of surfaces meet exactly. When this conjunction occurs let us say their force is not added one's to the other's but multiplied the one's by the other's; thus three or four words in exact juxtaposition are capable of radiating this energy at a very high potentiality; mind you, the juxtaposition of their vertices must be exact and the angles or "signs" of discharge must augment and not neutralize each other. This peculiar energy which fills the cones is the power of tradition, of centuries of race consciousness, of agreement, of association; and the control of it is the "Technique of Content," which nothing short of genius understands.[12]

To charge the words with the maximum energy involves the poet's perspicuous understanding of "the power of tradition, of centuries of race consciousness, of agreement, of association." This in turn raises our question: the relation of *logopoeia* to the "dynamic content?" The concept of *logopoeia* has given considerable trouble to the critics. Some take it to

[12] "I Gather the Limbs of Osiris," *New Age*, x.13 (January 25, 1912), 298.

mean "wit" of the Augustan kind. William Empson takes it to mean a sort of verbal ambiguity. J. P. Sullivan, rejecting these explanations, suggests that it means "a refined mode of irony."[13] All of them have ignored this earlier unreprinted piece of criticism by Pound and have drawn their conclusion from the sources which Pound wrote and published much later. It seems to me that *logopoeia* is clearly the "Technique of Content" redefined:

> LOGOPOEIA, "the dance of the intellect among words," that is to say, it employs words not only for their direct meaning, but it takes count in a special way of habits of usage, of the context we *expect* to find with the word, its usual concomitants, of its known acceptances, and of ironical play. It holds the aesthetic content which is peculiarly the domain of verbal manifestation, and cannot possibly be contained in plastic or in music.
>
> *LE*, 25.

We now understand that the "state of mind of the original author" is constituted by the "power of tradition, of centuries of race consciousness, of agreement, of association." To a translator, the first act of translating should start with his entering into this consciousness and becoming aware of it. The second act of translating is to reproduce this consciousness by manipulating the "power of tradition, of centuries of race consciousness, of agreement, of association" inherent in the language translated into. But no two cultures can be identical, hence the impossibility of total cultural translation. Naturally, there are parts (words, phrases, images, names and allusions) not reproducible *ad verbum*. The translator can and sometimes should follow the general outline and progress set in the original poem, but his important role as a "bridge-maker" lies *not* where he can annotate those unreproducible

---

[13] See J. P. Sullivan's *Ezra Pound and Sextus Propertius* (Austin, Texas, 1964), pp. 64-67.

parts in terms of the "tradition, race consciousness, agreement and association" of the original language, but where he can improvise upon those parts to obtain corresponding effects that can be *expected* (see quotation above) in the "tradition, race consciousness, agreement and association" of his *own* language.

Milton became the main object of Pound's attack (starting with *The Spirit of Romance*, 1910) because he falls short of this *double consciousness*, and Arthur Golding has been held up as a model for translation because he does not.

> Milton undoubtedly built up the sonority of the blank verse paragraph in our language. But he did this at the cost of his idiom. He tried to turn English into Latin; to use an uninflected language as if it were an inflected one, neglecting the genius of English, distorting its fibrous manner, making schoolboy translations of Latin phrases: "Him who disobeys me disobeys. . . ." The sin of vague pompous words is neither his own sin nor original. Euphues and Gongora were before him. The Elizabethan audience was interested in large speech. "Multitudinous seas incarnadine" caused as much thrill as any epigram in *Lady Windermere's Fan* or *The Importance of Being Earnest*. The dramatists had started this manner, Milton but continued in their wake, adding to their high-soundingness his passion for latinization. Golding in the ninth year of Elizabeth can talk of "Charles his wane" in translating Ovid, but Milton's fields are "irriguous," or worse, and much more notably displeasing, his clause structure is a matter of "quem's," "cui's," and "quomodo's."
>
> MIN, 109-110; LE, 238.

Arthur Golding, meanwhile, has nothing "fustian" in his translation and "his *Metamorphoses*," according to Pound, has formed "possibly the most beautiful book in our language." *MIN*, 110n.:

I am not insisting on "Charles his wane" as the sole mode of translation. I point out that Golding was endeavoring to convey the sense of the original to his readers. He names the thing of his original author, by the name most germane, familiar, homely, to his hearers. He is intent on conveying a meaning, and not on bemusing them with a rumble. And I hold that the real poet is sufficiently absorbed in his content to care more for the content than the rumble; and also that Chaucer and Golding are more likely to find the *mot juste* . . . than were for centuries their successors, saving the author of *Hamlet*.

MIN, 110; LE, 238.[14]

Apart from the emphasis on the translator's awareness of the potentialities of the words in both languages, this mode of translation, namely "Charles his wane," implies the necessary improvisation by the translator upon the parts not readily available to his audience. For the same reason, Pound thinks that "obscurities due not to the thing but to the wording, are a botch, and are not worth preserving in a translation." By

---

[14] Although this essay was written in 1917, about three years after the date of the translation of *Cathay*, Pound had assumed this position as early as 1912. A key passage that Pound liked to repeat in his prose will show this: "La poésie, avec ses comparaisons obligées, sa mythologie que ne croit pas le poète, sa dignité de style à la Louis XIV, et tout l'attirail de ses ornements appelés poétiques, est bien au-dessous de la prose dès qu'il s'agit de donner une idée claire et précise des mouvements du coeur; or, dans ce genre, on n'émeut que par la clarté." (Stendhal) Pound comments: "And that is precisely why one employs oneself in seeking precisely the poetry that shall be without this flummery, this *fustian* à la Louis XIV, 'farcie de comme.'" (Italics mine) This is found in "The Serious Artist." (1912, *LE* 54) The entire passage from Stendhal was quoted again, with the same emphasis, in a note of homage to Wilfred Blunt (January 1914) in *Poetry* III. 1, p. 223. The words "fustian" and "farcie de comme" reappeared in other essays. Cf. *GB*, 146-47; *LE*, 238; *MIN*, 160. In fact, this emphasis is not only in tune with his involvement in the movement against rhetoric (cf. Chapter II), but was well articulated in a series of essays he wrote for *The New Age* entitled "The Approach to Paris." *New Age*, XIII.19-25 (September-October 1913).

extension, the parts that are not essential to the original author's consciousness can sometimes be excised, provided such an act does not alter the original consciousness.

2

When we turn from Pound's theory of translation to his execution in *Cathay*, everything that he said in his theory seems to be playing against him. We find, for instance, that Pound did not know any Chinese at that time and the English cribs he got from Fenollosa prove, in some cases, faulty and difficult.[15] Pound admitted in his letter to Katue Kitasono in 1937 (*Letters*, 293) that he had no inkling of the technique of sound in the Chinese original, which he was later "convinced *must* exist and have existed in Chinese poetry." How is it possible for him to be aware of the "tradition, race consciousness, agreement and association" of the original? (We can, of course, take it for granted that he is fully aware of these elements in the English language). Hence, Roy Earl Teele criticizes the concept of translation by collaboration as exemplified by Pound-Fenollosa, Lowell-Ayscough, and Bynner-Kiang:

> It is as difficult to imagine that the distinctions between Li Po's style and Li Yü's style could be made clear to someone without any knowledge of Chinese. . . . It would be possible of course to describe the differences in considerable details, if the assistant happened to be a sound literary scholar. Even so, such a description would be somewhat

---

[15] It was Hugh Kenner who first made it known to us that Pound has never dealt with the Chinese characters directly, but has always followed a crib (English, French, Latin). See "Ezra Pound and Chinese" *Agenda*, IV (October-November), 38-41. Achilles Fang's "Fenollosa and Pound," *Harvard Journal of Asian Studies*, XX.2 (June 1957), 213-38, is earlier, but he never pointed out that Pound did not deal directly with the characters.

like a description of differences between the paintings of Matisse and Cézanne for a color-blind person.[16]

Without being aware of Pound's theory of translation,[17] Teele seems to have criticized even his insistence upon conveying the *sense* as a mode of translation. Following I. A. Richards in his *Mencius on the Mind*, Teele thinks that the crib has all the defects that a dictionary has, i.e. you get only the sense, *not* the intention, feeling, and tone (all four terms are from Richards).[18]

This is fierce criticism, for it is, in a sense, a criticism of Pound by Pound himself (even though, as we understand, Teele did not know Pound's theory of the "Technique of Content"). Here, Pound seems to be trapped. This is, in fact, where most philological translators can, with pride and authority, dismiss Pound as a translator of Chinese.

But the interesting thing about Pound as a translator in this case is that, with all these limitations, he sometimes gets over in English a translation not only philologically accurate, but aesthetically right. Indeed, one can point out scores of mistakes in his translation, as, for example, those outlined in "Fenollosa and Pound" by Achilles Fang. One can also say, as did Arthur Waley, that the "Exile's Letter" is at most a brilliant paraphrase[19] and that Pound has indeed taken too much liberty in improvising that poem. (Compare my almost "literal" translation in Appendix II; Pound did not follow the syntax of the lines as he did in the other cases.)[20] And yet,

---

[16] Teele, *Through A Glass Darkly* (Ann Arbor, 1949), p. 6.

[17] It seems clear from the materials he consulted that he has not read the unreprinted essays of Pound, which are more important in this case than the pieces in his collected essays.

[18] Teele, p. 5.

[19] Waley, *The Poetry and Career of Li Po, A.D. 701-762* (London-New York, 1950), p. 11.

[20] Again we do not know if Pound was actually following an already improvised crib by Fenollosa.

83

strangely enough, Pound has occasionally (by what he calls "divine accident"?) penetrated below a faulty crib to the original and come out right. This happens in "The Lament of the Frontier Guard," i.e. Li Po's "Ku Feng (After the Style of Ancient Poems) No. 14."[21] To make it convenient for our discussion, let me give my own translation first:[22]

1 The barbarian pass is filled with windblown sand
2 Squalling from ancient times till now.
3 Trees stripped of leaves, autumn grass goes yellow.
4 We climb up to look over the barbarous land:
5 Desolate castle, vast empty desert,
6 No wall left to this frontier village,
7 White bones lying across a thousand frosts,
8 Huge mounds, covered by thorns and brushwoods.
9 Who is the aggressor? Let me ask.
10 The barbarians' malicious martial move
11 Has brought the emperor's flaming anger.
12 He ordered the army to beat the war-drums.
13 Calm sun turned into murderous air.
14 He called for soldiers, causing a turmoil over the
    Middle Kingdom.
15 Three hundred and sixty thousand men.
16 Sorrow, sorrow, tears like rain.
17 Grief-drenched, yet we had to go.
18 How are we to farm our fields?
19 Without seeing the frontier men

[21] Fenollosa annotated this poem under a Mr. Hirai whose knowledge of Chinese is obviously less dependable than Mori Kainan's. Mori Kainan was not only a distinguished scholar of Chinese in Japan, but a renowned *kanshi* poet (i.e. a Japanese writing poetry in Classical Chinese). I am indebted to Hugh Kenner and Mrs. Dorothy Pound for Fenollosa's notes on this poem. Two lines of this manuscript are reproduced in Kenner's "The Invention of China," *Spectrum* IX.1 (Spring 1967), 48-49.

[22] I have tried to keep this translation both literal and readable. To make it a "poetic" translation, I might have to strike off a few things.

20 Who would know the dreary sorrow at the pass?
21 General Li Mu is no longer here.
22 We guardsmen fed to tigers and wolves.

For line 2, which literally may be rendered "bleakness and loneliness (suggested by the rustling of dried grass) reaches (or exhausts, or ends with) antiquity," Fenollosa gives us this:

| a kind of reed called in Japan "ogi" = the shape of the wind. "a red wife" [?] | rough | at length | end | old |

everything coming to its end and becoming old as if withered by the wind.

There is nothing here that quite resembles the original. Fenollosa, or perhaps Hirai for that matter, did not even understand that the first two words are meant to be a compound, meaning the sound of leaves or grass blown by autumn wind, suggesting bleakness, dismalness, loneliness, etc. But notice how Pound emerges from Fenollosa. The endless bleak and lonely aspect of the site is well preserved:

1 By the North Gate, the wind blows full of sand,
2 Lonely from the beginning of time till now!

For line 6, which, in word-for-word order, is "border/ village/ no/ left-behind/ wall," Fenellosa has

| side | village | not | leave | fence |

The villagers which are far from the capital—i.e. on frontier—have no fences left for them (fig.): have no defenders.

This is muzzy annotations. Pound restores the word "wall" in place of "fence":

6 There is no wall left to this village.

thus keeping the original metaphorical function intact.

The next few lines (10, 11, 12) are even more dramatically resurrected. It is worth quoting this part fully:

Heaven   angry   poison   might   martial
            (full of spirit   (good
            like wild horse) meaning)

Heaven was angry and inspired martial power:
            necessary to use strong medicine—inject it

red   rage   our   sage   Emperor
            angry

Our Emperor became red with anger

tire   teacher   matter   hi   ko
to soothe   general of   = becomes   a kind   ordinary
the tired   the army   the matter,   of drum   drum
                                is done   beaten on
                                                horseback
                                                = a certain kind
                                                   of music

To soothe the army it became a main matter of the Emperor to employ music

86

All these glosses over glosses serve no purpose but to confuse the translator. A bare skeleton of the original in word-for-word order will be helpful here:

10 Heaven's-pride (the Huns, the barbarians)/ malicious/ martial/ warlikeness
11 awful(ly)/ anger(v.)/ our/ holy(majestic)/ emperor
12 labor(v.)/ army/ employ/ war-drums.

The "barbarians" ("Heaven's pride," a name for the Huns seen in the *History of Han*) is absent from Fenollosa, not to mention the apparently erroneous and confusing glosses. Line 12 gives a meaning almost entirely opposite to the original. The purpose of the drums is to "inspirit" rather than to "soothe" the army. Fenollosa's mistake is due to his misunderstanding of the first two characters of that line which simply means "to order the army." Yet Pound, either through intuition or through careful research of his own, restores for the English readers something close enough to the "power" and "effect" of the original:

9 Who brought this to pass?
11 Who has brought the flaming imperial anger?
12 Who has brought the army with drums and with kettle-drums?
10 Barbarous kings.

The words "barbarous kings" are brilliantly re-introduced into Fenollosa's crippled text to help complete the "inner thought-form" that is emerging from the somewhat chaotic details. Although Pound has reversed the order of the images by turning the flat statements into questions of dramatic suspension, any sensitive reader of poetry would probably hesitate to charge him for this improvisation. Instead of diverting the readers from the "essential poem," the new arrangement has actually intensified the same sentiments. It builds up a crescendo in rhythm, a rhythm of considerable suspension, by letting the second line break the quantity of the first line and terminates this accelerating and expanding tension with an answer of the abrupt and almost brutal finality of a gong. And Pound has not deviated significantly from the original, as the hopeless English crib might easily have led him to do. Kenner, without reference to the original, considers "barbarous kings" Pound's own invention to give balance to the other lines.[23] He did not know that Pound in this case actually penetrated beneath the literal surface and resurrected what Fenollosa had missed from the original.

One can easily excommunicate Pound from the Forbidden City of Chinese studies, but it seems clear that in his dealing with *Cathay*, even when he is given only the barest details, he is able to get into the central consciousness of the original author by what we may perhaps call a kind of clairvoyance.

In a similar vein, we find Pound producing these lines from "The River-Merchant's Wife: A Letter" (i.e. "The Song of Ch'ang-kan"):

1 While my hair was still cut straight across my
forehead
2 I played about the front gate, pulling flowers.
3 You came by on bamboo stilts, playing horse,
4 You walked about my seat, playing with blue plums.
5 And we went on living in the village of Chokan:
6 Two small people, without dislike or suspicion.
7 At fourteen I married My Lord you.
8 I never laughed, being bashful.
9 Lowering my head, I looked at the wall.
10 Called to, a thousand times, I never looked back.

Arthur Waley was apparently very unhappy with Pound's translation, and he decided to show Pound a few things by re-translating some of Li Po's poems that Pound had rendered. These are found in a paper he read before the China Society

[23] *Spectrum*, 48.

at the School of Oriental Studies, London, on November 21, 1918.[24] One of these efforts is "Ch'ang-kan." This is how he rendered the above lines:

1 Soon after I wore my hair covering my forehead
2 I was plucking flowers and playing in front of
   the gate,
3 When you came by, walking on bamboo-stilts
4 Along the trellis, playing with green plums.
5 We both lived in the village of Ch'ang-kan,
6 Two children, without hate or suspicion.
7 At fourteen I became your wife;
8 I was shame-faced and never dared smile.
9 I sank my head against the dark wall;
10 Called to, a thousand times, I did not turn.[25]

What we consider good in Waley is already forged in Pound, for instance, line 10. "Called to, a thousand times, I did not turn," can hardly be considered Waley's own nor does it show any improvement upon Pound's "Called to, a thousand times, I never looked back." The gesture of "looking back" (or of her refusing to look back) which helps to vivify the visualization of her shyness and which in turn makes the entire picture even more lovable than it is, is totally lost in Waley's "I did not turn." One may argue that Waley is more literal,[26] for the line in question is, word-for-word, "thousand/ call/ not/ one/ turn(-head)." But in translation, one should

---

[24] The paper is entitled *The Poet Li Po A.D. 701-762*, East and West Ltd. (London, 1919). It is also published as an article in *Asiatic Review* (October 1919), 584-610. It was Achilles Fang who first pointed out that this was a "shot meant for Pound." See Fang, p. 221n.

[25] *The Poet Li Po A.D. 701-762*, p. 18.

[26] Waley has endorsed the theory of literal translation. Cf. *170 Chinese Poems*, Third Printing, p. 33. But there are two levels of literal translation, one being the reproduction of the mode of representation by attending to the syntactical literalness (to which I subscribed in Chapter I), the other being the transmission of the prose sense or dictionary sense alone.

89

always go beyond the dictionary sense. And here Pound does and Waley does not. This is even truer in line 1 and line 6. Line 1 in word-for-word translation is: "'My' (humble term used by women when speaking of themselves)/ hair/ first/ cover/ forehead."

WALEY: Soon after I wore my hair covering my forehead
POUND: While my hair was still cut straight across my
forehead

Pound has crossed the border of textual translation into cultural translation and Waley has not, though he is close enough to the original. Whether the credit for the phrase "hair . . . still cut straight across" should go to Fenollosa or to Pound's own observation in Laurence Binyon's Department of Oriental prints and drawings in the British Museum is of no important consequence here. What is important is that this picture is culturally true, because the characters for "hair/ first/ cover/ forehead" conjure up in the mind of a Chinese reader exactly this picture. All little Chinese girls normally have their hair cut straight across the forehead.

Even more stimulating than this visual recreation of cultural details, which restores flesh to the skeleton of dictionary meanings, is Pound's ability to go beyond the "word-sense" and "phrase-sense" and capture the voice and tone of the speaker, something which no dictionary can ever provide and which it takes a student years of familiarity with the language to grasp. Waley translates line 6, "two/small (children)/no/ hate/ suspicion," into "Two children, without hate or suspicion." It is obvious that he is accurate in the sense that he has not changed a bit from the given dictionary meanings. Yet Pound, keeping close to the dictionary meaning, has done something more:

Two small people, without dislike or suspicion.

It is indeed difficult to describe in another language the tone

HIS "MAESTRIA" IN TRANSLATION

and attitude with which the two characters (兩 小) (two/small) are spoken. However, we can at least say this: it implies that a grown-up person is speaking to a person (an imaginary audience) about two children's innocence. And in this case, the wife is speaking to herself and her husband together (imagining that her husband is actually before her) about themselves in the phase of innocence (imagining that they both now see themselves, as children, in front of them). There is a peculiar aura of intimacy, love, and hushed beauty around these two characters as they are being spoken, one that can only be shared by the addressee who forms a part of this lovely scene. Now, Waley's "two children" has of course conveyed the idea of innocence, but being merely a statement of fact, it does not assume the tone of a grown-up person speaking, with love and intimate playfulness, to and before a child. Pound's "two small people," harking back to the vocabulary of nursery rhymes, seems to me to have fulfilled all the demands described above.

To turn from these specific contours of consciousness to the more general meanings in the poem, we find that Waley has unjustly translated "bamboo-horse" into "bamboo-stilts." A bamboo-horse is something like a hobby-horse or cockhorse as in a nursery rhyme which begins

>Ride a cockhorse to Banbury Cross
>To see a fine lady on a white horse.

Chinese children like to use a bamboo-stick (without the horse-head) and make believe that it is a horse. They ride on it the same way one would ride on a cockhorse. Pound also uses "bamboo-stilts" (which form another favorite game for Chinese children but are different from a bamboo-horse), but keeps the horse-image.

Waley deliberately changes the word ("bed") into "trellis," and gives in a footnote this explanation: "It is hard to believe that 'bed' or 'chair' is meant, as hitherto translated. 'Trellis'

91

is, however, only a guess." (p. 18) But, as well illustrated by Charles Patrick Fitzgerald in his recent book *Barbarian Beds; the Origin of the Chair in China* (1965), the Chinese character in question can be a bed (primary meaning), a chair, a seat, or a couch. And since they were mere small children, there is no reason why they should avoid playing around a chair, seat, or even a bed. (In fact, one might even suspect that the word "bed" is used deliberately to evoke simultaneously two sorts of memories, that of distant childhood and that of recent past, for the addressee is the speaker's husband.) Pound, probably trying to avoid erotic connotations,[27] chooses "seat" for "bed," which is closer to the original than Waley's choice. It could be more specific.

There is also a level of formality in the lines involved which Waley misses and which Pound retains. One word in line 1 (妾) (literally, concubine, a humble term used by women or wives when speaking of themselves) and one word in line 7 (君) (lord, you) reflect the two levels of formality in the forms of address between husbands and wives that were commonly maintained at that time (the eighth century). Pound, without overdoing it, retains this flavor in the line

7 At fourteen I married My Lord you.

The honorific level here implies that the speaker is addressing from a humble level.

It seems quite clear now that although Pound has been sharply limited by his ignorance of Chinese and by much of Fenollosa's crippled text, he possesses a sense of rightness, an intuitive apprehension in poetic organization or, to borrow a term from Eliot, "the creative eye"[28] which we should not be-

---

[27] Is it possible that for the same reason Pound has changed the last line in "The Beautiful Toilet" which goes "Empty bed! Alone! How hard it is to keep" into "And leaves her too much alone," in order to maintain better taste?

[28] Eliot, *Sacred Wood* (London, 1920), p. 77.

grudge giving due credit. For even within the limits of free improvisation and paraphrase in the "Exile's Letter," he sometimes tends to come closer in sensibility to the original than a literal translation might. I give here the ending of that poem in my almost "literal" translation:

> You asked me how much sadness I know:
> Falling flowers at spring dusk bustle in confusion.
> To talk about it? There is no end.
> To spell my emotion? There is no word.
> I call my son to kneel down and seal this letter
> And send it to you, a thousand miles, and thinking.

Waley has it:

> And should you ask how many were my regrets at
>   parting—
> They fell upon me thick as the flowers that fall at
>   Spring's end.
> But I cannot tell you all—could not even if I went
>   on thinking for ever,
> So I call in the boy and make him kneel here and
>   tie this up
> And send it to you, a remembrance from a thousand
>   miles away. (1950)[29]

And Pound has it:

> And if you ask how I regret that parting:
> It is like the flowers falling at Spring's end
>   Confused, whirled in a tangle.
> What is the use of talking, and there is no end
>   of talking,

---

[29] *The Poetry and Career of Li Po* (London-New York, 1950), p. 15. Waley meant, of course, to show Pound how much he has deviated from his literal translation. A closer comparison between the two versions will indicate how much he is indebted to Pound's version for his phrasing and that he has been directed by Pound in wrestling with the thought progress in that poem.

There is no end of things in the heart.
I call in the boy,
Have him sit on his knees here
    to seal this,
And send it a thousand miles, thinking. (1915)

3

In the "Ku Feng No. 14" (i.e. "Lament of the Frontier Guard") two planes of action, each pursuing its full course, are at work, one cutting into the other, one defining the other until they converge in a node. "When this conjunction occurs . . . their force is not added one's to the other's, but multiplied the one's by the other's . . . radiating . . . energy at a very high potentiality."[30] These two planes are the barbarity of the natural world and the barbarity of the human world.

The time of the year is the devastating autumn in the north of China when the cutting wind not only makes a turmoil of the sand upon the vast desert, but murders the grass, taking away its life-color, and the trees, stripping them of their leaves. If there were a controller of all this, he did not notice what was happening before him, for, it seems, he had nothing to do with it.

What is happening is ruthless killing. The lust for land has knocked down castles and walls, has stripped bodies of flesh, laying bone heaps in waste and has caused a turmoil by soldiers over the entire kingdom. If there were a spirit behind all these actions, he, too, had paid no heed to the brutal season.

The wind has blown from the beginning of time till now and it will blow on.

The killing has been done from the beginning of time till now and it will go on.

---

[30] From Pound's discussion of the "Technique of Content" in *New Age*. See note 11 and text quoted.

The cruel season is meant, of course, to be the counterpart of the brutal human world. As Pound once remarked, there is a peculiar beauty in this unstated resemblance and the beauty is the result of "planes in relation"; they are beautiful "because their diverse planes overlie in a certain manner." (*GB*, 146)[31] But as in Pound's "In a Station of the Metro," the two planes do not stay forever on a parallel. They could be bound together, for instance, by what Pound has called "the language beyond metaphor," or by a sort of emotional or inner correspondence achieved, for example, when the word "black" merges into the word "apparition" in the Metro poem. (See Chapter II) There is still another way in which they can become what Eliot has called "complete consort dancing together."[32] This is by letting the two planes merge into "a radiant node or cluster . . . a Vortex, from which, and into which, ideas are constantly rushing." (*GB*, 106) And the "node" in Li Po's poem (the original) is in the line

陽 一 和 變 殺 氣

| the principle of *yang*, i.e. active, positive | harmony | change | killing | air |

This is a perfect line in which to show that dictionary transcription is destined to fail to convey the full connotations of the words. There is first involved in the line a philosophical and cosmological concept, the principles of *yin* and *yang* in the phrase "positive harmony," which is normally annotated as "the breath of spring." The principles of *yin* and *yang*, derived from the ancient *Book of Changes* (*I Ching*), explain

---

[31] See Chapter I.
[32] From Eliot's "Little Gidding" in *Four Quartets*. See Pound's definition of LOGOPOEIA as "the dance of the intellect among words."

the origin of the universe. To avoid cumbersome annotations and re-annotations of this concept, let us here quote from the summary of its meanings by a contemporary historian of Chinese philosophy, Fung Yu-lan:

> The word *yang* originally meant sunshine, or what pertains to sunshine and light; that of *yin* meant the absence of sunshine, i.e. shadow or darkness. In later development, the *yang* and *yin* came to be regarded as two cosmic principles or forces, respectively representing masculinity, activity, heat, brightness, dryness, hardness, etc. for the *yang*, and feminity, passivity, cold, darkness, wetness, softness, etc., for the *yin*. Through the interaction of these two primary principles, all phenomena of the universe are produced.[33]

It is not exactly "interaction" that is involved, but "cooperation," i.e. one complements the other in producing the world, according to the *Book of Changes*.[34] But instead of "cooperation" for the act of creation, the active, life-giving breath of *yang* is now turned into the air of killing. The phrase "killing/ air" (殺 氣) is intriguing, but exact and powerful. For besides being a phrase descriptive of warfare, it was first used to describe the inclement autumn. Even more interesting is the fact that it was used to mean also the breath of *yin*. The phrase was found in a chapter on the seasons in *Lü-shih Ch'un-chiu*, a compendium of different schools of philosophy in ancient China around the third century B.C. attributed to Lü Pu-wei, which later formed the "Yüeh-ling" ("Monthly Commands") chapter in *Li Chi* (or *Li Ki*, the *Book of Rites*):[35]

---

[33] Fung, *A Short History of Chinese Philosophy*, ed. and trans. by Derk Bodde. (New York, 1962), p. 138.

[34] *Ibid.*, p. 169.

[35] Pound had not read the *Li Ki* translated by Couvreur until he wrote *Canto 52* (Fang, p. 237) which is based on this chapter. He did

是月也〔仲秋之月〕.....殺氣
浸盛，陽氣日衰

(This/month (mid-/autumn/'s/month) . . . killing/air/
soak/full,/*yang*-/air/daily/ wither.)

In Couvreur's hand:

En ce mois [au deuxième mois de l'automme] . . .
Le souffle de la mort devient de plus en plus
puissant; le souffle de la vie décroit châque jour.[36]

"Le souffle de la mort" should be "the air of killing," and "le souffle de la vie" should be "the breath of *yang*."[37] The fact that the former is put in diametric position with the latter suggests that "the air of killing" is also "the air or breath of *yin*," as indeed it was so annotated by Kao Yu of the Later Han Dynasty (A.D. 25-200).

Hence the phrase "killing/air" at once subsumes a triple association, first with the principle of *yang*, but playing ironically against it, acting as its complementary principle of *yin*; then with the barbarity of the natural world and with the brutality of the human world.[38]

---

not, however, choose this particular detail for his *Canto*. He gives us this:

This month is the reign of Autumn
Heaven is active in metals, now gather millet
      and finish the flood-walls
Orian at sunrise.
                  Horses now with black manes.
Eat dog meat. This is the month of ramparts.

[36] Couvreur, *Li Ki* (Ho Kien Fou, 1899), i, 383.
[37] This is no criticism of Couvreur's translation. It aims only to clarify the phrases in question.
[38] Both for historical and cosmological reasons, the dual reference of the phrase has been observed by most poets. Ts'en Ts'an (circa 744), for instance, has written these lines: "Upon the terrace, the in-

We can see here how this phrase can, without twisting its meaning, be justly called "a radiant node" (if not the "vortex" which has wider historical connotations), from which, and into which, the two planes of action—natural and human barbarity—are rushing.

This is, of course, very much in tune with Pound's own temperament, for it fulfills all the requirements put forth in his "Technique of Content," and the energy comes exactly from "the power of tradition, of centuries of race consciousness, of agreement, of association" and from "ironical play."

The problem now lies in how much of this consciousness is given Pound in Fenollosa's notes on this line. As we can expect, they are hopelessly bare:

positive	mild	change	kill	gas
outside				miasma

(=yo, principle
of spring
The mild clear principle turned into a poisonous vapor.
(denotes the state of people at the coming battle.)

The key term in the line that has dual reference to inclement autumn and to warfare is represented here by "kill/gas" (gas!) or "miasma," which can lead the translator to practically anywhere but the right connotations. It is amazing that from these notes Pound has managed to give us

A gracious spring, turned to blood-ravenous autumn

Without the exact counterpart in Western cosmology of the the principle of *yin* and *yang*, it becomes flatly impossible to capture the overtones of the phrase "positive/harmony," even if the cosmology behind these two Chinese characters was made known to Pound. The most one can do, therefore, is to

clemency of frost attacks the vegetation/ In the army the 'air of killing' surrounds the banners."

retain the dual reference and forego the verbal ironical play. Judging Pound with this in mind, "blood-ravenous autumn" seems magnificent. For the word "autumn," which is neither in the original line nor in Fenollosa's notes, is exactly the thing to which the "air of killing" refers, and, without Pound's knowing it, "blood-ravenous" is almost a perfect translation of the phrase (killing/air/soak/full) from which the phrase "killing/air" in the original is taken. We can, of course, call this an accident, but what a divine one! The important thing is, to be exact, that it allows the two planes of action—natural and human barbarity—to merge together, as is true of the original.

At this point, it is perhaps relevant to answer the charges that have been or could be made against Pound. Pen-ti Lee and Donald Murray (a collaboration again!) have considered "Trees fall, the grass goes yellow with autumn" (l.3)[39] a mistranslation, which, from a philological point of view, is indeed true. The trouble with their criticism of Pound is that they have neither consulted Fenollosa's manuscripts (two examples were given by Chisolm in 1963, one by Noel Stock in 1965), nor have they familiarized themselves with Pound's poetry and criticism. For if they had known both, they would have drawn quite different conclusions.

Fenollosa's notes show that his annotations of that line coincide with Lee and Murray's interpretation ("Li Po's words meant 'the trees fall the leaves,' i.e. cause them to fall," p. 269):

木	落	秋	草	黃
tree	fall	autumn	grass	yellow

The tree leaves fall, and autumn grass is yellow.

[39] "The Quality of *Cathay*: Ezra Pound's Early Translations of Chinese Poems," *Literature East and West* x.3 (September 1966), 269. Although they claim to do more than A. Fang's cataloguing of mis-

Pound's change of this line into "Trees fall, the grass goes yellow with autumn" is deliberate and for an artistic reason. The central consciousness of the poem is, as we now know, the double brutality or barbarity confronting the poet. "Trees fall" is violent, as Lee and Murray charged; but has this "violence" outstripped that of the season and that of killing or has it enhanced the "energy" of the central consciousness as a whole?

Lee and Murray overlooked another interesting philological mistake. Line 5, in Fenollosa's hand, reads

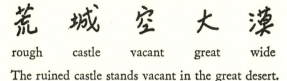

| rough | castle | vacant | great | wide |

The ruined castle stands vacant in the great desert.

A closer approximation would read (though in awkward English) like this:

Deserted castle; empty vast desert

Pound renders this into

Desolate castle, the sky, the wide desert

Ignoring Fenollosa's crib, one can easily charge Pound for having read the Chinese character for *vacant* (空 *k'ung*) (in this context, *empty*) for *sky*, in another context. Reading it against the crib now, we understand this is another change for artistic intensity. It aims at deepening the desolation and loneliness by projecting the desolate castle (a point) upon the wide desert (an endless stretch ending in a circle) and below the sky (another endless stretch ending in a circle), adding a dimension of height and a corporeal reality to the desolation

---

takes, one will find, on closer examination, that they have not, for they fail to treat them as poetry. They seem to lack consciousness of the "dynamic content" of either the original or the translation.

and loneliness. The difference between the original and Pound's modified line is that the former still has a chance of being considered as merely part of the visual objects in cataloguing sequence, while the latter seems to take hold as a self-sufficient image.

One can, of course, argue that when a translator tends to improve what is before him, he immediately stops being a translator *per se*. We can easily accept this argument. But if a translator, by such "violation," has actually intensified or solidified rather than violated the central consciousness of the original poem, can we not say that moving beyond dictionary transcription is perhaps more indispensable to the art of translation than staying always close to it?

Pound has indeed made many philological mistakes as a consequence of his ignorance of Chinese. But it is important to remind readers that not all of them are due to ignorance; many are done deliberately to heighten artistic intensity, and some, for a less defensible reason, are conditioned by his own obsessions as a practicing poet. These we will point out as we move on to the discussion of other poems.

It is an illuminating experience to see Pound breaking through verbal barriers into the core of the poem, but we must not forget that we are dealing with a Homer whose eyesight has been blocked by many physical hindrances, not to mention that even Homer himself sometimes dozed off. Therefore, in his many efforts to reach to the different forms of consciousness behind the poems in *Cathay*, and although they emerge triumphantly as poetry, some of the translations are hard-earned.

chapter four

In Search of Forms of Consciousness

In his essay "On the Relation of Analytical Psychology to Poetic Art," Carl G. Jung discriminates between two processes of artistic activity. He thinks that certain works proceed from the author's intention and others flow spontaneously from his pen. The procedures involved in the execution are necessarily different.

> Thus we should expect in the former case, that nowhere would the work transcend the limits of conscious understanding, that its effect would, as it were, be spent within the author's intention and that in no way would its expression exceed the author's deliberate purpose. In the latter case we should have to conceive something of a supra-personal character that transcends the range of conscious understanding in the same degree as the author's consciousness is withheld from the development of his work. We should expect a certain strangeness of form and shape, thoughts that can only be apprehended by intuition, a language pregnant with meanings, expressions that would have the value of genuine symbols, because they are the best possible expressions of something as yet unknown—bridges thrown out toward an invisible shore.[1]

If we admit this distinction between conscious and unconscious art as a valid one, we will find that translation always

[1] Carl G. Jung, *Contributions to Analytical Psychology*, tran. H. G. and Gary F. Baynes (London, 1928), p. 239.

proceeds from the limits of conscious understanding. Unlike the unconscious artist, the translator is not free to drift with his materials. He is constantly compelled to make a choice from among the different possible intentions behind the original poem and to determine the "state of mind" embodied in it, whether or not the poem in question flows spontaneously from the author's pen. Hence Pound writes, ". . . having *determined* the original author's state of mind, you may or may not be able to find a derivative or equivalent." (*LE*, 25. Italics mine) The choices translators make in front of a text ultimately yield differing forms of consciousness in their translations. We have a living example in Pound's own translations from the Chinese. The first poem in *Cathay*, "Song of the Bowmen of Shu," was retranslated by Pound into Ode 167 in *The Classic Anthology*. The "Song" is a reworking from Ariga's English version.[2] At that time Pound was entirely ignorant of the technique of sound[3] in the original and had not even seen the format of the original. When he translated the Odes, he had already accumulated a certain amount of knowledge about the relation of these poems to music, although he was still following a crib, this time a much more dependable one by Bernhard Karlgren. Accordingly, he consciously rendered the Ode in the form of a ballad,[4] something we do not find in the "Song." By adding this dimension to the Ode, Pound has given us a form of consciousness quite different from that in the "Song." Let me give here the first stanza of this poem in its different metamorphoses:

[2] See Hugh Kenner's report, "Ezra Pound and Chinese," *Agenda*, IV (October-November 1965), 38.

[3] *Letters*, p. 293.

[4] See also Donald Davie, *Ezra Pound, Poet as Sculptor* (New York, 1964), pp. 38-39. Although Davie discusses these two versions without reference to the original, his conclusion about their metrical differences is valid and illuminating.

103

采	薇	采	薇	(mi̯wər)
薇	亦	作	止	(tsâk ti̯əg)
曰	歸	曰	歸	(ki̯wər)
歲	亦	暮	止	(mâg ti̯əg)
靡	室	靡	家	(kâ)
玁	狁	之	故	(ko)
不	遑	啓	居	(ki̯o)
玁	狁	之	故	(ko)

pick/ fern/ pick/ fern
fern/ (expletive)/ sprout/ (expletive)
(expletive)/ return/ (expletive)/ return
year/ (expletive)/ dusk(v.)/ (expletive)
no/ house/ no/ home
Hsien/ yün/ 's/ cause (Because of Hsien-yün)
no/ time/ kneel/ sit (i.e. rest)
Hsien/ yün/ 's/ cause

(My approximation:

1 Pick ferns, pick ferns,

2 Ferns are sprouting.

3 Return, return,

4 The year is dusking.

5 No house, no home,

6 The Hsien-yün are the sole cause.

104

7 No time to rest,
8 The Hsien-yün are the sole cause.)

Song:

1.2 Here we are, picking the first fern-shoots
3.4 And saying: When shall we get back to our country?
5.6 Here we are because we have the Ken-nin for our foemen,
7.8 We have no comfort because of these Mongols.

Ode:

1.2 Pick a fern, pick a fern, ferns are high,
2.3 "Home," I'll say: home, the year's gone by,
5.6 no house, no roof, these huns on the hoof.
7 Work, work, work, that's how it runs,
8 We are here because of these huns.[5]

The eight-line stanza is rendered into four lines in the "Song" and five lines in the "Ode." But except for the fourth line, the "Ode," enforced by internal rhymes, actually reads like this:

Pick a fern, pick a fern,
ferns are high,
"Home," I'll say: home,
the year's gone by,
no house, no roof,
these huns on the hoof.
Work, work, work, that's how it runs,
We are here because of these huns.

[5] Translations by other people will be brought into focus later in this chapter. For Ariga's version and Karlgren's crib, see Appendix I. The rhymes beside each Chinese line are transcribed in accordance with their archaic pronunciation reconstructed by Karlgren.

From a rhythmic viewpoint, the "Ode" is closer (except for some over-stretching of the meaning, for instance, in line 7) to the original than the "Song,"[6] which, for lack of such rhythmic demarcation, proceeds in the manner of a narrative.

This comparison reveals one fact: the "indestructible" part that Pound could obtain from Fenollosa's uneven notes for the poems in *Cathay* hinged heavily on his consciousness of the "cuts and turns"[7] of the mind in the poems rather than on his awareness of their rhythmic structures. The rhythm of these poems is largely superimposed and can hardly be considered an approximation of the original. In other words, the "equivalents" in *Cathay* are forms of consciousness that Pound has reproduced with exclusive emphasis upon the "internal thought-form." As such, Pound's version of Li Po's "Ku Feng No. 14" (i.e. "Lament of the Frontier Guard") is successful because he has grasped surprisingly well the cuts and turns of Li Po's mind in the poem (see Chapter III) in spite of the fact that he is trapped in a crippled text. In the following pages, we will attempt to anatomize, as it were, the "internal thought-form" of the other *Cathay* poems and see how Pound goes about recasting these "cuts" and "turns" in his "equivalents," and how his translations sometimes break down into mere "derivatives" or Poundian poems in face of an insufficient crib.

[6] I have no intention to extend this judgment to the other odes in that *Anthology*. Pound is sometimes very associative in translating some of the poems there.

[7] This phrase is borrowed from Gene Fowler's "Brainwashing, Hypnogogic Recall and An Approach to Poetics," *Trace*, Nos. 62/63 (London-Hollywood, Fall-Winter 1967), 251, which is not a study of Pound. However, I find it quite illuminating for the present purpose. The sentence from which this phrase is taken reads: "We tend toward a kind of filmic imagism . . . toward the cuts and turns that are like the movements of living minds."

The Topoi of the "Complaint of the Frontier Guard"

In Li Po's "Ku Feng No. 14" (see Chapter III) we find that the dominant cause of the guardsman's complaint is the doubled barbarity—natural and human—he is confronted with. His complaint ranges from the bleakness of the place (North China) and the destructiveness of autumn to the eerie sight of bone-heaps and relentless killing in battle. Inclement winds and snow, coupled with hazards of blustering sand, form another source of his complaint. In face of these cruelties that stretch indefinitely into his future, he pines for spring and home that are denied him. These motifs are released in the progression of a semi-monologue. A semi-monologue may be defined as a form of address at once to the speaker himself and to a concealed or absent audience. Most of the time the speaker would address inwardly to himself, but he would suddenly turn outward and speak to an imaginary audience, expecting, in his tone and attitude, a response from it. Such an assumption immediately establishes some sort of dramatic interaction between the speaker and the listener, but the response is furnished by the speaker himself; hence the address remains essentially a monologue. Thus the line

借 問 誰 陵 虐

(line 9   Who is the aggressor? Let me ask . . .)[8]

is not literally asked by an audience, but by the speaker himself who goes on to give an answer. This "inner monologue" (to be exact, "inner dialogue") moves easily into a rhythm akin to lyrical trance (Pound's "inner form of the line"?) without relying on the external sound structure of the poem.

[8] For my translation of the whole poem, see Chapter III and Appendix II.

107

When I recapitulate these motifs and elaborate on the view-point of the guardsman's complaint, I aim at clarification of the underlying structure of all the poems about the complaint of the frontier guardsmen which form a sizable portion of Chinese poetry. But even more interesting is the fact that the germ of this type of poetry begins with "Pick Ferns, Pick Ferns" which is also the first poem in *Cathay* (i.e., "Song of the Bowmen of Shu"). Both the motifs and the viewpoint in all the subsequent "complaint" poems of this kind are largely prepared by this ode. To facilitate our discussion of this poem, let me give here my own approximation:

1 Pick ferns, pick ferns,
2 Ferns are sprouting.
3 Return, return.
4 The year is dusking.
5 No house, no home,
6 The Hsien-yün are the sole cause.
7 No time to rest,
8 The Hsien-yün are the sole cause.

9 Pick ferns, pick ferns,
10 Ferns are soft.
11 Return, return,
12 Hearts are sorrowful.
13 Sorrowful hearts burn, burn.
14 Now hunger, now thirst.
15 Garrison here and there,
16 No message home.

17 Pick ferns, pick ferns,
18 Ferns are coarse.
19 Return, return,
20 The tenth month is here.
21 King's affairs still undone,
22 No time to rest,

23 And sorrow pierces heart.
24 We go and return not.

25 What is blooming?
26 Flowers of the cherry.
27 Whose imposing chariot?
28 The general's.
29 War-chariot is yoked,
30 Four horses so tall.
31 How dare we settle?
32 One month, three battles.

33 Ride the four horses,
34 Four horses martial in gait.
35 The general rides behind.
36 Beside them, lesser men.
37 Four horses, a grand file.
38 Ivory bow-ends, fish-bone arrow-holders.
39 How dare we slake?
40 The Hsien-yün are wide awake.

41 When we set out,
42 Willows dangled green.
43 Now I return.
44 Sleets in a mist.
45 We drag along.
46 Now hunger, now thirst,
47 My heart is full of sorrow.
48 Who knows? who will know?

Although, as we see here, there is no mention of bleakness of place, no depiction of bone-heaps and death, and no elaboration on sand and wind hazards except perhaps the encounter with "sleets in a mist," the poem still largely corresponds to Li Po's "Ku Feng" (i.e. "Lament . . ." in *Cathay*) in motifs and standpoint. We have, for instance, the stress on the doubled cruelties of the hard life ("pick ferns" to eat; "No house, no home"; "No time to rest"; "Now hunger, now thirst") and hard fight ("One month, three battles"; "How dare we slake/ The Hsien-yün are wide awake"), the emphasis on the duration of the frontier garrison and the denial to the soldiers of the privilege of home (Ferns sprout—grow soft—and coarse; "no message home") and their longing ("When we set out,/ Willows dangled green"). The poem progresses like a folk ballad with the characteristics of parallel constructions and repetitions, but the viewpoint of the speaker is that of a semi-monologue. There is a certain amount of dramatic directness in such lines as:

Pick ferns, pick ferns

Return, return

What is blooming?
Flowers of the cherry.
Whose imposing chariot?
The general's.

However, similar to the situation in Li Po's poem, both the presence and the response of the audience here are fictive, for the exchange of conversation is done by the speaker himself. And yet, because of the dramatic illusion set up by the questions and answers, the speaker is not bound by the logic of sequence and standpoint. He can move easily away from his standpoint to assume those of others (though imaginary ones). In this way, the speaker of the semi-monologue becomes the center of consciousness into which and out of which both his narrations and descriptions, both his dramatic assertions and plain statements, can move freely.

In the "Lament of the Frontier Guard," the cuts and turns of mind are projected into two planes of action cutting into one another and defining one another until they, by dint of their inner correspondence, converge into a "node." In this poem, the semi-monologic consciousness of the speaker be-

110

comes the switchboard that holds and releases simultaneously gestures and expressions of disparate experiences. And because of this fact (rather than because the Chinese language does not have clear tense distinction), it is important to see that in translation the tense for the most part should remain eternally present.

James Legge, for whose Chinese scholarship I have great respect and admiration, has unfortunately missed this central mode of consciousness and has, accordingly, not only incurred in his translation stylistic awkwardness but raised problems of coherence. Legge explains the viewpoint he has adapted in a footnote to his version of this ode:

> Though intended to encourage the departing troops, it [the ode] is written as if it were their own production, giving expression to their feelings on setting out, and in the progress of the expedition, down to its close. A translator's great difficulty is to determine the moods and tenses he will introduce into his version. "The Complete Digest" says, "The piece was made with reference to the time when the expedition was despatched, and the language throughout must be taken as that of anticipation. . . ." I have adapted my translation to this peculiarity.[9]

[9] *The Chinese Classics*, iv.ii (Hong Kong, 1871), 258-59. Legge makes it very clear that this was not his own view, but one he adapted from "The Complete Digest," see Legge, iv.i, 176 by Tsou Sheng-mo published in 1763. This viewpoint is quite orthodox, for the phrase

詩作於方遣之時，大抵皆是預道之辭耳

shih tso yü fang ch'ien chih shih, ta ti chieh shih yü tao chih tz'u erh
(Legge: The piece was made with reference to the time when the expedition was despatched, and the language throughout must be taken as that of anticipation)

is derived from the authoritative *Mao-Shih Chu-su* or *Mao's Explanations of the Shih Ching* with commentary by K'ung Ying-ta in A.D. 642 in the *Annotations with Commentaries to the Thirteen Classics* (*Shih-san-ching Chu-su*) via Yen Ts'an's *Shih-chi* or *A Commentary*

As a result his first stanza reads:

1 Let us gather the thorn-ferns, let us gather
  the thorn-ferns;
2 The thorn-ferns are now springing up.
3 When shall we return? When shall we return?
4 It *will be* late in the [*next*] year. [Sic.]
5 Wife and husband will be separated,
6 Because of the He'en-yün
7 We *shall have* no leisure to rest
8 Because of the He'en-yün.

(Italics mine)

---

of the Shih Ching from All Sources, 1248, in which many of Mao's long-winded explanations were abridged. Among the books Legge consulted, he said he made very frequent reference to Yen's book. The phrase in question was first coined in Yen's book. It appears in it twice with slight change in wording:

但采薇是遣之之始, 預道其勞苦

tan ts'ai-wei shih ch'ien chih chih shih, yü tao ch'i lao k'u

而囚以勉之

erh yin i mien chih

(Literally: But "Pick Fern" was [written] at the beginning of the despatch, anticipating their [i.e. the frontier guardsmen's] hardships so as to exhort them.)

—*Shih-chi*, Vol. 17, p. 24a

采薇方遣行之初而豫道其將

ts'ai-wei, fang ch'ien hsing chih ch'u erh yü tao ch'i chiang

來之勞苦見深體之心也

lai chih lao k'u, chien shen t'i chih hsin yeh

(Literally: "Pick Fern" [was written] at the beginning of the despatch and anticipated their future hardships, reflecting [King Wen's] deep thoughtfulness of them.)

—*Shih-chi*, Vol. 17, p. 28b.

And his last stanza reads:

41 At first, when we set out,
42 The willows *were* fresh and green,
43 Now, when we *shall be* returning,
44 The snow *will be falling* in clouds.
45 Long and tedious *will be* our marching;
46 We *shall* hunger; we *shall* thirst.
47 Our hearts are wounded with grief.
48 And no one knows our sadness.

(Italics mine)

This view is implied in Mao's explanations, first in the phrase

故歌此采薇以遣之

ku ko tz'u ts'ai-wei i ch'ien chih

(so sang this "Pick Fern" to despatch· them)

and then in many such phrases as

文王將以出伐豫戒役期云

Wen Wang chiang i ch'u fa, yü chieh i ch'i yün

(King Wen was about to send the soldiers on the expedition, and warned them ahead of time [of the hardships] of the active service)

故豫告行期

ku yü kao hsing ch'i

(so as to tell them ahead of time the duration of the expedition)

throughout the explanatory text. (See *Mao-Shih Chu-su*, Vol. IX.3, 10-16.) In fact, Legge's opinion that this ode and the two succeeding ones, Ch'u kü (Legge's title: "Ch'uh keu") and Ti tu (Legge's title: "Te too") form a triad is based on Mao.

Legge's translation is no doubt the most accurate according to the orthodox view, and hence, an invaluable academic document which no Chinese scholar can afford to ignore, but as a literary monument, his version lacks critical insight of the integrity of the poem from its inner structure. For even in his retranslation of this poem in 1876 in a volume designed to be *poetry* and not *document*, i.e., *The She King, translated in English Verse*, in which he could have been freer with

113

The word "[next]" in line 4 is awkward and serves no purpose for effective poetic communication. The tenses in the last stanza are ridiculous, for even if this is an anticipated situation, it is still necessary to assume an imaginary present (hence, the use of present tense) in order to stress the vividness of the actions. For the same reason, the "historical present" is often employed in a narration of past actions. In the making of a true lyric, the directness constituted by the present tense, and particularly by that of the semi-monologue, should be considered a major factor.

James Legge (p. 259) also believes that each stanza represents a different detachment sent out at different times of the year (on the basis of the growth of the ferns). Such a view is quite destructive, because the sorrow (or complaint) built up by the *duration* of their hard life and hard fight will be absent. Instead of escalating toward the platonic form of sorrow, this view tends to make each stanza the information of an incomplete and fragmentary sorrow.

At this point, it is interesting to find that both Ariga's version (for the most part) and Pound's "Song of the Bowmen of Shu" do not commit these breaches. Both versions employ the present tense. Although the monologic revelation of de-

---

orthodox interpretations, he maintained the future tense. The first stanza of the 1876 version reads:

> Come pluck the ferns, the ferns sharp-pointed take;
> The curling fronds now their appearance make.
> And now we march. O When shall we return?
> Till late next year we must in exile mourn.
> So long the husband, parted from his wife,
> *Shall* 'gainst the Heen-yun *wage* the deadly strife.
> 'Mid service hard all rest *will be denied*;—
> Northwards we go, to quell the Heen-yun's pride. (p. 198)
> (Italics mine)

Apparently, Legge already noticed the uneasiness caused by the different tenses in his other version, for in this new effort, he dropped the future tense in many cases and replaced it with more dramatic utterance.

tails in these versions is not as dramatic as it should be, we have in Pound's lines a certain amount of directness of address:

> What flower has come into blossom?
> Whose chariot? The General's.

These lines are derived from Ariga's

> What is that blooming flower?
> Whose is that chariot? That is our general's.

We notice here that in both versions one line is left out, namely, "Flowers of the cherry" in answer to the question "What is that blooming flower?" This is Ariga's fault.[10] The absence of an answer to this question leaves the line dangling, for the demonstrative adjective (in Ariga's interrogative line) exacts an immediate answer to complete the sequence of thought. Having no answer to work with and determined not to let the line falter like Ariga's, Pound changes it into a less definite and more tentative "What flower has come into blossom?," adding to the speaker's mood a level of uncertainty which is in tune with the mode of monologic revelation. The line as Pound has it could mean "I do not know what flower has come into blossom at home," or "I do not know what flower has come into blossom on the barren fields." It is true that it greatly deviates from the original and yet, in a sense, it has enhanced the monologic consciousness in the poem.

The loss of many motifs and much of the dramatic directness is also due to Ariga's crib. For instance, the line "No

[10] The conclusion made here is based on Ariga's version as printed in Chisolm's book, the only version available at present. I suspect, however, that something might have gone wrong in the process of transcription from the original manuscript, judging from the disorderly manner in which Fenollosa copied down the glosses and annotations. The missing line could very well be there in the original manuscript, but, being either placed like a marginal note or mixed with other explanatory notes, it might have been misunderstood as not being part of the poem proper.

house, no home" (in Waley, "We have no house, no home"; in Pound's "Ode," "no house, no roof . . .") is contracted by Ariga into

> Here we are *far from home* because we have the "ken-in" as our enemy.
>
> (Italics mine)

which suggests neither the directness nor the motif. However, the backbone of the different motifs—the doubled cruelties of hard life and hard fight—is preserved, in fact, not only preserved, but intensified at the risk of violating the original details. Before we examine how Pound alters Ariga's lines, it is instructive to look at the position both James Legge and Ariga have assumed in reproducing the part in question.

Mr. Legge explains in his notes that the expedition is made by the troops in a public spirit:

> Sze-ma Ts'een [Ssu-ma Ch'ien] in his Record of the House of Chow [Chou], and of the Heung-noo [Hsiung-nu, the Huns], says that in the time of King E (933-909 B.C.), those northern tribes became very troublesome, and refers to this ode as a composition of that time.—It is understood that this reference to the cause of the expedition is made by the troops in a public spirit, showing that they sympathized with the court in the necessity of taking it. (p. 259)

Ariga is following a text the annotations of which endorse this same position:

> (At the epoch of the last emperor of the "In" [i.e. Yin] dynasty, there appeared the two powerful barbarian tribes who often invaded the empire, namely: "Kon-i" in the western part, and "Ken-in" in the northern part of China proper. Bunno [i.e. Wen-wang or King Wen of Chou Dynasty] was the commander in chief of the western princes; he had to dispatch his army to defend against the

outsiders under the order of the emperor. In that time he composed this piece, as if he was one of the soldiers, to show his sweet sympathy to them and to soften their grief and pain. As the commander was so kind, the soldiers were glad to serve in his army. This is one of the chief reasons why the "Shu" [Chou] [Sic] dynasty arose and Bunno was esteemed as a saint.)[11] (See Appendix I.)

Accordingly, Ariga has reproduced for us these lines:

[11] This view in which the elements of "public spirit," "sympathy," and "willingness" to fight are involved, is basically that of Mao. Ariga, like Legge, might have followed Yen Ts'an's abridged version of Mao's view, for his explanation reads like a free translation of the beginning paragraph of Yen's exposition of Mao's text. The Chinese, in literal translation, runs:

采薇 ("Pick Fern," the poem) 遣戍役也 ([is about] despatching frontier guardsmen) 文王之時 (King Wen's time) 西有昆夷之患 (in the west border there was trouble caused by the K'un-i [Ariga's "Kon-i"]) 北有玁狁之難 (in the north, that caused by the Hsien-yün [Ariga's "Ken-in"]) 以天子之命命將率 (on behalf of the Heaven's Son, [King Wen] issued order to the commanders) 腰日天子殷王也 . (Commentary: *Heaven's Son is the Emperor of the Yin Dynasty*) 遣戍役以守衛中國 (to despatch frontier guardsmen to guard China) 故歌采薇以遣之 (so sang "Pick Fern" to despatch them).

Up to here all is quoted from the text of Mao. It continues with the following commentary and a general conclusion:

上能察其情 (Commentary: [*Since*] *the Above* [*i.e. Heaven's Son as well as King Wen*] *can understand and sympathize their feelings*) 則雖勞而不怨 (*although hard,* [*they had*] *no complaint*) 雖憂而能勵矣 (*although sorrowful,* [*they were*] *exhorted and encouraged into action*) ..... 采薇出車杕杜諸詩 (The poems "Pick Fern," "Ch'u kü," "Ti tu") 周之所興也 ([reflect] the reasons for the rise of the Chou Dynasty).

(Italicized parts are commentaries)
Shi-chi, Vol. 17, p. 23b.

We must be prudent for our affair (which is the order
of the emperor); we have no leisure to sit down
comfortably.
Our sorrow is very bitter, but we would not return
to the country.
What is that blooming flower?
Whose is that chariot? That is our general's.
The horses are hitched already to the chariot; they
seem to be vigorous.
How dare we repose? We must conquer the enemy even
three times a month.
Those four horses are tied; they are very strong.[12]

Pound, obsessed by the sorrow *itself*, has greatly modified the
soldier's "willingness," and "sympathy" as well as the grandios-
ity of the general's appearance:

There is no ease in royal affairs, *we have no comfort.*
Our sorrow is bitter, but we would not return to our
country.
What flower has come into blossom?
Whose chariot? The General's.

[12] Compare the word-for-word annotation of this part:
king's/ affairs/ not/ faulty (service to king
                    must not be defective)
no/ time/ kneel/ sit (i.e. rest)
sorrowful/ heart/ very/painful
I/ go/ not/ come
that/ blooming/ is/ what
is/ cherry/'s flower
that/ chariot/ is/ what
general/'s/ chariot
war/ chariot/ already/ harnessed
four/ horses/ tall-and-big
how/dare/ settle/ rest
one/ month/ three/ clashes
ride/ that/ four/ horses
four/ horses/ martial-in-gait

118

Horses, his horses even, are tired. They *were* strong.
We *have no rest*, three battles a month.
By heaven, his horses are tired.
(Italics mine)

We have no reason to believe that Pound misread *tired* for *tied* in the last line quoted, for two lines earlier he has changed *hitched* to *tired*. He did all this to reinforce the platonic form of sorrow. The emphatic "By Heaven" is purely Pound's and is nowhere found in the original.

It is quite apparent here that the form of consciousness Pound has reproduced for us is at least different in degree, if not in kind, from the original. In his deliberate effort to expand the shell of sorrow itself, he has sacrificed or violated some of the external details. The question we have to ask here is: does this violation change significantly the course of the poem? More specifically, what is the poetic function of the depiction of the general's grandiose appearance and should the details in that depiction receive as much emphasis as Ariga has given them? Indeed the general's grandiose appearance could serve to mark the distance between the soldiers and the people of higher ranks resulting from the former's respect for the latter, and the stress upon "prudence" (Ariga) and "faultless service" to the king (Legge and Karlgren) could mean "public spirit," "sympathy," and the soldiers' "willingness" to fight for the cause. But what seems to me more important is the fact that the shift to the general's grandiose appearance occurs only after the building up, in three stanzas, of the complaint about the hard life of a frontier guard. This flight into pomposity both relieves and contrasts with the hardships of the soldiers. In other words, this bursting into external description has turned the mounting sorrow subterranean until it comes out piercingly again in the atmosphere of a most miserable moment.

Now the proportion Ariga's version (probably due to his neglect of the stanza length) has given to these details has

119

entirely outstripped that of the brewing of the sorrow. This seems most inappropriate for a poem of complaint. Between "sorrow" and "public spirit," Pound has chosen the former to give the proper emphasis.

I think it would be preposterous to say that Pound's "Song of the Bowmen of Shu" has followed closely the curves of the original's internal thought-form, for we do miss in it the leap into an external action of lively tempo (Pound's alterations make it seem sluggish) and the undercurrent of sadness. And I think, although it is Ariga's fault, Pound has to admit that he has changed partially the character of the semi-monologue he has all the way dominated. Reading this poem (the original) is like coursing on a stirring stream when suddenly it turns underground. The voyager is compelled to travel on land, still remembering the stirring of the water. He later rejoins the stream which has then become turbulent. In Pound's version, the voyager is led slowly but directly into that turbulence. With this figure, I hope to make it clear that Pound's version has manipulated the central consciousness—the semi-monologic mode of revelation—quite well, but it has not been able to approximate the double movements that occur in the midst of the course; it is, therefore, different, in degree, from the original form of consciousness.

IF "Pick Ferns" stresses the semi-monologic mode of revelation, "Ku Feng No. 6" ("South-Folk in Cold Country" in *Cathay*) tends to give prominence to the motifs. The poem begins, for instance, with the place name Tai (代 , in North China) which rings with echoes of relentless killing. Tai was not just a place famous for horses as it is normally annotated, but a place brimming with memories of blood and death. Tai, Yen-men (Wild-goose Pass 雁門), and Yün-chung (雲中), linked with a long defensive wall constructed by King Wu-ling of Chao (307 B.C.),[13] had been for centuries the targets of constant attacks by the barbarians:

The Hsiung-nu (Huns) grew more arrogant day by day, crossing the border every year, killing many of the inhabitants, and stealing their animals. Yün-chung and Liao-hsi suffered most severely, while in Tai Province alone over ten-thousand persons were killed.[14]

This is only one of the earliest records (166 B.C.). Countless attacks of this kind were to follow for hundreds of years. Meanwhile this region also recalls famous generals who fought the Hsiung-nu, among them Li Mu (Pound's "Rihoku"> "Riboku" in "Lament of the Frontier Guard," died 288 B.C.), Li Kuang, the Winged General (Pound's "Rishogu">"Rishogun" in his version of this poem, died 125 B.C.)[15] and Wei Ch'ing (died 113 B.C.), the general-in-chief. In this region and further north from there, these generals had their endless garrisons and hard fights, and were defeated and captured (e.g., Li Ling in the year 99 B.C.).

To complete the diptych of brutality, we have the natural barbarity:

Startling sand confounds the sun above the "Vast
    Sea" (i.e. Gobi Desert)
Flying snow bewilders the barbarian sky.

[13] Ssu-ma Ch'ien, *Shih Chi* (*Records of the Grand Historian of China*), trans. Burton Watson, 2 vols. (New York-London), ii, 159.
[14] *Ibid.*, ii, 173.
[15] Pound has given this information about Rishogun in his *Cantos*:
    And Li-kouang bluffed the tartars (the Hiong-nou)
        in face of a thousand, he and his scouts dismounted
    and unsaddled their horses, so the Hiong-nou
        thought Li's army was with him.
                                                    54/24
The story is also found in *Shih Chi*. See Watson, ii, 145.

To match these defenders' "hard fight," there are the voices about their "hard life":

Lice grow inside helmets and mails.
Our spirit is driven with the silken banners.

To give full utterance to their "complaint," their address is direct and unreserved instead of the ambiguous and subtle expression of "public spirit":

Hard fight earns no imperial reward.
Royalty is difficult to express.
Who would pity the Winged General Li,
Who, white-headed, was lost among the three
    border states?

(Translations are mine)

The reader should have noticed by now a very disturbing fact: that I have to resort to annotations outside the text to make the poem fully understandable. In order words, I have to re-supply, by way of pedantic prose, an "accompaniment"[16] or, to be exact, glosses, to make the readers aware of the "mental content"[17] of the audience of a different culture. Can we translate *poetically* all these echoes and associations coming from the reservoir of "race consciousness"[18] (in the Chinese language) into English? To put it differently, how are we to translate allusions without employing annotations? Some form of improvisation is called for. The first lines in Waley's version are for specialists:

[16] See Pound, Introduction to "Cavalcanti Poems," *Translations*, p. 7: "It is conceivable the poetry of a far-off time or place requires a translation not only of word and of spirit, but of 'accompaniment,' that is, that the modern audience must in some measure be made aware of the mental content of the older audience, and of what these others drew from certain fashions of thought and speech."

[17] See note 16.

[18] This is Pound's own phrase. See his definition of the "Technique of Content" in Chapter III.

122

The T'ai horse cannot think of Yüeh;
The birds of Yüeh have no love of Yen.
Feeling and character grow out of habit:
A people's customs cannot be changed.[19]

The readers are expected to know at least that Tai (Waley's T'ai) and Yen were in the north and Yüeh was in the south. Nor can my version (which is intended to indicate line structure for the sake of comparison) claim to have translated the "accompaniment." Replacing Waley's "T'ai horses" by "North-born horses," it has perhaps a small merit of suggesting barely the bleak North, part of the details being provided by subsequent lines. (For my whole translation, see Appendix II.)

What complicates the situation for Pound is that such an "accompaniment" is not provided for at all in Fenollosa's notes, not to mention the numerous mistakes he has glossed. Fenollosa's glosses for the first four lines follow on page 124.

These lines promise nothing "poetic." No information of the echoes and associations that the Chinese audience would be aware of is here provided for Pound to work with. Although the parallelisms have a rhetorical interest for the Chinese audience, they mean no more than four lines of unnecessary repetitions to Pound. And even if the rhetorical structure had been known to Pound, I strongly doubt that he would have observed this verbal play, not only because he advocated a movement to kick out rhetoric and make way for *vers libre*, but because he has written obsessively about the question of local "taste" in translation: "If a work be taken abroad in the original tongue, certain properties seem to become less apparent, or less important. Fancy styles, questions of local 'taste,' lose importance. Even though I know the over-whelming importance of technique, technicalities in a foreign tongue cannot have for me the importance they have to a man writing in that tongue." (*MIN*, 160) For this reason, the 16 elaborate

[19] *The Poet Li Po, A.D. 701-762*, p. 12.

代	馬	不	思	越
Dai	horse	not	think	Etsu

The horse of Dai does not think (much of) Etsu

越	禽	不	戀	燕
Etsu	bird	not	love	swallow

The bird of Etsu does not love swallow

(Dai is a place famous for horses
Etsu is a place famous for certain kind of birds)

情	性	有	所	習
Feeling	character	is	place	learn

Each feeling and character (of a thing) depends upon
the place of its custom

土	風	固	其	然
Earth	wind	originally	that	like

Air of earth (i.e. local habit) is originally [illegible]
like that

and tightly-packed parallel lines from Lu Chao-lin's "The
Old Idea of Ch'ang-an" were broken up by Pound into 32
short and long lines of no distinct parallelisms. (Compare
Pound's "The Old Idea of Choan" to my approximation in
Appendix II.) For the same reason, the four lines here are,
on the contrary, contracted into three. Two lines give the
essential meaning—nature and feeling are born of habit and
to go against this truth is to breed suffering:

2 The birds of Etsu have no love for En, in the North.
3 Emotion is born out of habit.

124

Pound adds the title, "South-Folk in Cold Country" to point out the situation.

The first line clearly departs from the given detail. Pound improvises it into

1 The Dai horse neighs against the bleak wind of Etsu.

Nowhere in the notes nor in the original can this particular figure be found. Could it be that he inferred this from the line (i.e. in Fenollosa's version),

The flying snow goes wandering over the wild sky?

Or could it be that, dissatisfied with Fenollosa's notes, he drew an analogy from the first lines of another "complaint" poem, "Lament of the Frontier Guard," which read, in Pound's hand,

By the North Gate, the wind blows full of sand,
Lonely from the beginning of time till now?
(See discussion in Chapter III)

Whatever it might be, he seemed to be sure that, by inserting the figure, he has not distorted the motifs that underlie this poem, but has given to it an added degree of "natural barbarity."

But what intrigues me most is the way in which Pound violates the sentence structure in the line

 沙 亂 海 日

| Startling | sand | derange confound | sea (i.e. sun above the "Vast Sea," ancient name for the Mongolian Desert) | sun |

The structure of this line is in the 2-1-2, i.e., subject-verb-object, relation (see Chapter I). Thus the line can readily be rendered as

Startling sand confounds the sun above the "Vast Sea"

or, as Waley puts it,

Startled sand blurs the desert sun.

Even Fenollosa's notes do not deviate from this structure, in spite of the fact that parts of the line are ambiguously and mistakenly annotated:

Surprise   sands   mix   sea   sun
This sand surprised confuses the sun rising out
    of the sea.

But Pound changes Fenollosa's line into

Surprised. Desert turmoil. Sea sun.

From a literal viewpoint, this has indeed changed drastically the original syntactical structure. Although the first two characters (startling/sand) do not necessarily form a compound, they are used here like a compound, the first character being a qualifier of the second character. These two characters become the subject of the verb "derange" (third character), which in turn takes the fifth character, "sun," as object with the fourth character, "sea" (abbreviation of "Vast Sea," ancient name for the Mongolian Desert), as its qualifier. Pound splits the subject, making the first character into an independent verb, while combining the second and the third, noun (subject) and verb, into a new compound, leaving the fourth and the fifth to make another group. Anybody who has some sense of the syntax of the Chinese language will be ready, at this point, to denounce Pound.

But there is no point in our pursuing the indictment further, for it seems that we have already caught him red-handed.

What concerns us here is whether such a misdeed has affected the character of the poem and if it has, how. More important still, we should go beyond the discussion of translation to see how Pound's own practice has conditioned the change.

In the discussion of both "In a Station of the Metro" and "Lament of the Frontier Guard" I brought out a peculiar trait of Pound's mind. We found him obsessed with a beauty achieved by having "diverse planes overlie in a certain manner" and with a technique to merge the planes into a "radiant node" by manipulating the inner correspondence of the words. We have also seen how Pound successfully manipulated these poems (one original English and one translation) to achieve these goals. It seems that the same obsession is at work here in his deliberate change of the lines in question.

Right after the lines "Yesterday we went out of the Wild-Goose gate,/ To-day from the Dragon-Pen,"[20] Pound isolates the word "Surprised," causing it to mean simultaneously "to be seized by the barbarians' unexpected attack" and "to be taken suddenly by the sandstorm." This word has become, like the phrase "blood-ravenous autumn" in "Lament of the Frontier Guard," the "node" into which two planes of action, relentless killing and natural hazards, merge. Moreover the word "Surprised" so placed not only allows two pictures to cut into each other, but also becomes a third one, namely the impression of bewilderment and disorder (a result of surprise attack), reinforced by the synchronous images of visual derangement,

> Surprised. Desert turmoil. Sea sun.
> Flying snow bewilders the barbarian heaven.

One impression is superimposed upon the other until it has become a composite and intense impression. Such an impression, spliced with various shots which are in themselves self-sufficient, is like a "rosette" formed by many circles whose

[20] These lines are from Pound's version.

arcs converge at a center. Or, to change the figure, the separate impressions are arcs of different circles continuously cutting into one another like the ripples formed by a stone dropped into the middle of the pond. This is the result of what Pound once called "super-position" (see Chapter I), but this is also the effect of cinematic montage, a device extensively employed in the *Cantos*.

Again it is obvious that although both the original and Pound's version are to focus upon the motifs, the form of consciousness in the latter is different in degree from that in the former. Although Pound did not deviate from the motifs that underlie this type of poetry, he intensified the impression of the doubled cruelties and, unlike what he did to "Pick Ferns," quickened the tempo by a device that had obsessed him even before he encountered the *Cathay* notes.

"Complaint of the Estranged Wife":
Ironical Play

While "Pick Ferns" furnishes Chinese poetry with the prototype for the frontier guard's complaint, "Ancient Poems No. 3" (second poem in *Cathay*) becomes the germ of another type of poetry, namely, "the complaint of the estranged wife." The theme summed up in the last lines of this poem,

> The playboy went and never returned.
> Empty bed! Alone! how hard it is to keep.
>
> > (Translation is mine)

has been copied, repeated, and varied. The wife is estranged by a playboy or by one who goes off to war in search of a position of rank. Estrangement, particularly over a period of ten years or more, naturally begets a deep sense of sadness.

But of all the poems that portray this sadness from estrangement, none is as well remembered as "Ancient Poems No. 3" and those that are equally proverbial show a structural principle that derives from this poem.

What, then, is this structural principle? For the sake of clarification, let us start with a poem modeled after "Ancient Poems No. 3." This is Wang Ch'ang-ling's (graduated A.D. 726) "Complaint from a Lady's Chamber":

> In the chamber the lady knows no sadness.
> Spring day, dressed up, she climbs a tower of jade.
> She sees suddenly the willows' green over the fields
> And regrets having sent her husband to search for
>   ranking positions.[21]

For comparative purposes, let us now look at a version that has reversed the thought progress:

> At the head of a thousand roaring warriors
> With the sound of gongs,
> My husband has departed
> Following glory.
>
> At first I was overjoyed
> To have a young wife's liberty.
>
> Now I look at the yellowing willow-leaves;
> They were green the day he left.
>
> I wonder if he also was glad?[22]

Let us also ignore the translator's deviation from the original details and focus on the process in which sadness unfolds. In the first version, if we were not given the fourth line, we would perhaps take it to be a vignette of an innocent person in her

---

[21] This is my own version. Waley's version reads:

> In her boudoir, the young lady,—unacquainted
>   with grief.
> Spring day,—best clothes, mounts shining tower.
> Suddenly sees at the dyke's head, the changed
>   colour of the willows.
> Regrets she made her dear husband go to win a fief.
>
>   *Chinese Poems* (London, 1916), p. 9.

For Fenollosa's notes, see Appendix I.

[22] Powys Mathers, *Love Songs of Asia* (New York, 1946), p. 62.

bloom of youth. In other words, she could indeed be the one that knows no sadness. But her catching sight of the willows' green, as is here heightened for us by the word "suddenly," has, without her preparedness, struck the hidden chord of sadness and shocked her into recognition of the emptiness that surrounds her and of the wretched state she put herself into out of naïveté. The flash of interest here is the interplay of irony and the doubled chord created by the reverse of the situation. If we are to take the last line as a pond of water reflecting a gorgeous city built up by the first three lines, the upside-down picture is completely disfigured, i.e., the lady ignorant of sadness is actually brimming with sadness, the sprightliness and high spirit with which she climbs up a tower of jade is now overwhelmed by an emotion that belies both the occasion ("spring day") and her appearance ("dressed up"), and the willow, a sign of spring, lively activity and re-juvenation, reminds her now of the moment of her husband's departure, during which (following the Chinese tradition) she was supposed to have broken a twig to present him as a parting souvenir.

In the second version, the reversed order of images has completely destroyed the subtle play of sadness against para-doxical gaiety. The discursive and annotative lines, "At first I was overjoyed/ To have a young wife's liberty" (which is the translator's insertion), take away all the dramatic effect of recognition.

Turning back to "Ancient Poems No. 3" (i.e. "The Beau-tiful Toilet" in *Cathay*), which is the prototype of Wang's poem, we can easily see the same ironical play at work. In fact, the process in which sadness unfolds in this poem is even subtler than the one we have discussed. Since Fenollosa's notes on this poem are, to our surprise, literally quite accurate, we will use them here but add the Chinese characters on top of every line, interpolating suggestions within square brackets where his notes might be misleading:

青
blue
[green]

青
blue
[green]

河
river

畔
bank
side

草
grass

鬱
luxuriantly
spread
the willow
[dense]

鬱
luxuriantly
spread
the willow
[dense]

園
garden

中
in
[middle]

柳
willow

盈
fill
full

盈
fill
full

樓
storied
house

上
on

女
girl

[in first bloom
of youth]

皎
white
brilliant
luminous

皎
white
brilliant
luminous

當
just
face
[at]

窗
window
[window]

牖
door

娥
beauty of
face
[adj.]

娥
beauty of
face
[adj.]

紅
red

粉
powder
(or berri)

妝
toilet

纖
slender

纖
slender

出
put forth

素
white
blank
not dyed

手
hand

131

昔	為	倡	家	女
in former times	was (did)	courtesan	house	girl

今	為	蕩	子	婦
now	is	dissipated [wandering] [vagrant]	son's	wife

蕩	子	行	不	歸
dissipated [wandering] [vagrant]	son	go away	not	return

空	牀	難	獨	守
empty	bed	hard	only one alone	keep

The play of sadness against paradoxical gaiety is too obvious to need elaboration. We are first led slowly to concentrate on the lady's youthful beauty and, suddenly, without our knowing, the tone and atmosphere is changed. Instead of using my approximation as a point of departure for our discussion, it is perhaps more interesting to see the difficulties I encountered, trying to reproduce the way the original builds up the impression of the lady's beauty to the point before the ironical shift.

It seems that the author, whoever he may be, takes a special point of view in laying out his details. He presents them in different phases of perception. He first notices the grass in the distance, next the willows in the garden (closer) and then the girl up in the tower (still closer) who becomes the center of the objects around her. This centripetal movement (the reduction of a circle to a point) continues. From the girl the poet moves to a most salient part, namely the face, and then to a specific part, namely the hand. The movement from the grass (on the circumference) to the hand (point) is characterized by an incremental change in the thickness of color and the intensity of light.

Now the change of color and light lies in the reduplications that begin the first six lines. The problem here is that sometimes each reduplication assumes several meanings and all of them can become easily a qualifier of the item following it. Are we to choose the meanings, in Waley's hand, "green/ green"—"thick/thick"—"sad/sad"—"white/white"—"fair/fair" —"small/small," or these: "green/green"—"dense/dense"— "full/full"—"bright/bright"—"flash(of fairness)/flash"—"slender/slender"? Neither can be really wrong. But if the accelerated impression of glamorous beauty means a climax to be undercut by the sadness that follows, the second order, or the approximation of it, seems to be more desirable. In fact, if we are to take the ironical play as the skeleton of the poem, then Waley's "sad/sad"[23] (line 3) should be considered as having let the cat out of the bag, for, emerging as it does in the middle of the ascent toward the climax, it has annihilated the whole drama. When the shift comes in line 7, it is *expected*

---

[23] The Chinese character is 盈 (*ying*), whose meanings gather around the idea of "fullness." Even though *ying* is also considered a borrowed word for another Chinese character 嬴 , it nowhere suggests "sadness." The authoritative Chinese dictionary to date *Dai Kan-wa Ji-ten*, ed. by Tetsuji Morohashi (1883—) has given the following meanings as understood from Chinese literary documents: (1) fill, (2) to be full, brim, (3) overflow, (4) lengthen, (5) sufficient, (6) [get or attain] as one pleases, (7) advance, (8) angry [rare], (9) much, (10) full [moon], (11) pretty, (12) surplus (VIII, 22961). This shows "sad" is Waley's guesswork or his deliberate change for an effect he wants to achieve. But the change, as we shall see, is not warranted either.

IN SEARCH OF FORMS OF CONSCIOUSNESS

rather than *unexpected*. But, as we understand it, *unexpectedness* rather than *expectation* is the clue of the poem.

The second problem involved here is that of English usage. Although reduplications have a peculiar rhetorical interest for the Chinese audience, they never work in an English poem. Hence Waley's approximation,

> Green, green,
> The grass by the river-bank. . . .

accurate as it is, is quite insipid. For the same reason, most of the reduplications in the *Cantos*, except in cases where special musical effects are emphasized, do not constitute a significant rhetorical interest for the English audience.

In order to transmit the effects of the change in thickness of color and intensity of light as well as the rhetorical interest in the reduplications, I have reproduced the following experimental version, keeping it literal for comparison:

1 Green beyond green, the grass along the river.
2 Leaves on leaves, the willows in the garden.
3 Bloom of bloom, the girl up in the tower.
4 A ball of brightness at the window-sill
5 A flash of fairness is her rouged face.
6 Slender, she puts forth a slender white hand.
7 She was a singing girl before,
8 Now wife of a playboy.
9 The playboy went and never returned.
10 Empty bed! Alone! How hard it is to keep.

Although the early Yeatsian repetitions[24] and Anglo-Saxon

[24] I have in mind particularly the structure of the following lines, all taken from *The Collected Poems of W. B. Yeats* (New York, 1940):
Flame to flame and wing to wing. (p. 42)
Who rise, wing above wing, flame above flame. (p. 49)
Flame under flame, till Time be no more. (p. 53)
For hours when all must fade like dew,
But flame on flame, and deep on deep,
Throne over throne where is half sleep. (p. 61)

134

alliterations I adopted have preserved a certain amount of the rhetorical interest as well as the peculiar phases of perception (green—leaves—bloom—brightness—flash—slender white hand), they have sophisticated the simplicity of the original reduplications. The readers are asked to focus more attention upon the change in color and light than required. And in order to achieve this effect, I am also compelled to make some changes, for instance, the reduplications in lines 2 and 3.

To turn now from this basic understanding of the poem in question to Pound's translation, we are in a better position to tell his merits and demerits.

The Beautiful Toilet

1 Blue, blue is the grass about the river
2 And the willows have overfilled the close garden.
3 And within, the mistress, in the midmost of her youth,
4 White, white of face, hesitates, passing the door.

6 Slender, she puts forth a slender hand;

7 And she was a courtesan in the old days,
8 And she has married a sot,
9 Who now goes drunkenly out
10 And leaves her too much alone.

We have subtler music here. Hugh Kenner has ably shown us the intricacy with which Pound has woven the reduplications into the lines. He says that although the poem begins by reduplicating,

it modulates immediately to a less obvious pairing:

And the *willows* have *over*filled the close garden.

The third line relies on paired m's and a clustering of short i's:

And w*i*th*i*n, the m*i*stress, in the m*i*dmost of her youth

The fourth returns to reduplication:

135

White, white of face, hesitates, passing the door.

The fifth line of the Chinese he omitted, taking from it only a title, "The Beautiful Toilet." From the sixth he made another reduplication, its members gracefully separated:

Slender, she puts forth a slender hand.[25]

Without Sino-Anglicizing the translation as Waley does, nor sophisticating the reduplications as my experiment has probably done, Pound's treatment appears to be quite satisfactory, for, by building the reduplications (or their equivalents) within the line, he has kept intact the natural breath of the English language.

What remains to be seen is whether Pound has at the same time preserved the ironical play of the original.

It is apparent that he understood the ironical play rather well, for he has done two things to emphasize this structure. First, the title "The Beautiful Toilet" taken from the fifth line enforces the paradoxical gaiety (compare "dressed up" in the other poem discussed earlier) which is to be undercut by the reversal of the situation. When Hugh Kenner says that Pound discarded this line because it is not usable,[26] he has missed this interplay. Second, Pound spaces out the last four lines, allowing the second impression to play against the one captured in the previous five lines and the title. To emphasize the change of state of our lady, he renders the plain statement of "The playboy went and never returned" into a dramatically visual image of violent behavior, "Who now goes drunkenly out," to play against the gentleness and tameness of our lady.

But we also see a difference between the original form of consciousness and the one contained in Pound's version. Partly misled by Fenollosa's notes, Pound has not followed the centripetal movement, and, as a result, has missed the incremental

[25] Hugh Kenner, "The Invention of China," *Spectrum* IX.I (Spring 1967), 23.
[26] Kenner, p. 33.

buildup of the impression of our lady's beauty. The change
of the intensity of light is lost. By using "within" (line 3)
instead of "up in the tower," Pound has created an outside-
inside relation of the details, not, as we would expect, the
reduction of a circle to a point. Although Pound has not let
the cat out of the bag the way Waley does, he has "hidden"
that possibility in the words "blue"[27] (which is partly Fenollosa's fault), "close" (line 2, suggesting estrangement), and
"hesitates" which turns the "white, white of face" into an
ambiguous impression: is "white" to mean "pale" or "pow-
dered" white? This prepared inner correspondence certainly
ties the poem together skillfully, but it has also affected
(though not as drastically as Waley's "sad/sad") the clue of
the poem which is an unexpected shift of the state of emotion.

Pound is always obsessed with the platonic form of emotion.
In "Song of the Bowmen of Shu," we have the "atom" of
sorrow; in the "South-Folk in Cold Country," that of "bewilderment"; in this poem, "sadness in loneliness." To attain this core, he tends to pare away the unnecessary implica-
tions. Take the line,

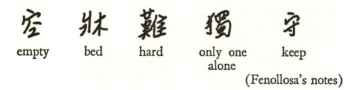

空	牀	難	獨	守
empty	bed	hard	only one alone	keep

(Fenollosa's notes)

It is hard to determine the degree of erotic association implied here, but nuances of it, however vague, are no doubt
there. Giles has, for instance, advanced this extreme interpretation:

[27] Although the character in question 青 covers the spectrum
from green, blue, to dark blue, it is usually understood as *green* when
applied to grass.

137

Ah, if he does not mind his own,
He'll find some day the bird has flown.[28]

While Giles' change has overstressed the nuances, Pound's version has eliminated them. Having "hidden" the sadness in the first half of the poem, he determines that the emotion must surge out in its pure being and so changes the line into

And leaves her too much alone.

The Platonic Form of the Poem

Pound's obsession with the pure being of the poem has led him to defy incommunicability by seeking freedom from limits of time and locale: "An 'Image' is that which presents an intellectual and emotional complex in an instant of time. . . . It is the presentation of such a 'complex' instantaneously which gives the sense of sudden liberation; that sense of freedom from time limits and space limits." (*LE*, 4) In order to hold on to the "indestructible" part of the poem, the poet is to abandon "local" taste (*MIN*, 160) because certain things can never be translated "locally." (*LE*, 25) This belief of Pound's is reflected in several of his translations. Take the case of Wang Wei's (A.D. 699-759, i.e. Pound's "Omakitsu") "To See Yüan Erh Off as Envoy to An-hsi." A word-for-word translation of this poem[29] reads:

1 Wei/City/ morning/ rain/ wet/ light/ dust
2 Inn/ house/green/ green/ willow/ color/ new
3 Advise/ you/ again/ drink-up/ one/cup/ wine
4 West/ out-of/ Yang/ Pass/ no/ old/ friend

Wei City here refers to the region (north of the Wei River) in which a great deal of military activity against the barbarians was carried out.[30] The departure calls up also a passage

---

[28] Giles, *History*, p. 98.
[29] At this point, Fenollosa's notes on this poem are not available.
[30] Ssu-ma Ch'ien, *Shih Chi*, trans. Burton Watson, II. 175-76.

from *The History of Han Dynasty* (*Han Shu*): "General Li Kuang-li was going to lead the army to attack the Hsiung-nu. The Prime Minister saw him off all the way to the Wei Bridge" (66/5a). The Yang Pass is the last pass to the barbarous land.

Both the locale and the time constitute an aura of associations that defy translation. Judging from Fenollosa's inability to provide the associations from the same source for the two frontier poems we have discussed, it is likely that he failed again in this instance. It is fairly certain that Pound was confronted with at least two names, Wei City and Yang Pass, about which he had to do something. And this is what he has given us:

1   Light rain is on the light dust.
2   The willows of the inn-yard
2a Will be going greener and greener,
3   But you, Sir, had better take wine ere your departure,
4   For you will have no friends about you
4a When you come to the gates of Go.

To Pound, the "indestructible" and "translatable" part of the poem is the "estrangement" resulting from separation. The *specific* time and *specific* space that constitute this *specific* situation certainly add a local flavor and significance to the consciousness of the Chinese audience. But before the merging of two cultures becomes a matter of common and wide acceptance,[31] these specific associations cannot be felt by the English audience except by educated readers (who are, at present, restricted only to sinologists and to some Chinese who happen to know English). The only thing that can be fully responded to by the English audience is the primary and essential emotion of "estrangement," i.e. when it is stripped of the cumbersome local associations. Thinking in these terms,

[31] The Japanese, for instance, can respond rather fully to these associations without resorting to erudite annotations.

Pound has omitted "Wei City" (I Chō in Japanese) completely from the poem and has turned "Yang Pass" (Yō kan) into the almost anonymous "gates of Go," subjecting everything to the platonic form of estrangement in the last line

4a For you will have no friends about you
4b When you come to the gates of Go.

It is quite possible that he has, for the same reason, suppressed the locale ("Yang-chou") and the time ("third month") in line 2 of "Separation of the River Kiang"[32] and has turned "Yellow Crane Tower" (line 1) into a fictive, anonymous Ko-kaku-ro.

Throughout all eighteen poems in *Cathay* Pound has not used one single annotation of the sort I have supplied here. One explanation is his ignorance of the "consciousness" of the Chinese audience, as most criticisms of Pound's *Cathay* tend to see. But has he not done more poetic justice to Wang Wei's poem than those who have neglected the double consciousness involved in the act of translation? To thrust upon the readers the first line of this poem, with or without annotations, as Jenyns has it

[32] From the notes on part of the poem now available (*Spectrum*, p. 33) and the format in which the poem is annotated (i.e. word-for-word), one can gather that neither "Yang-chou" (yō-shu) nor "third month" would be left out in the manuscript.

The mistake of making Kiang (=river) a proper name has already been pointed out by Lee and Murray. (*LE & W*, p. 270)

As to the reason for changing "old acquaintance" (that is, in Fenollosa's notes) deliberately into "Ko-jin," quite possibly, it is for musical effects. Ko-jin appears also in Wang Wei's poem and in "Taking Leave of a Friend." Pound translates it into "friends" in the first case and "old acquaintances" in the second. He could not have misunderstood Ko-jin (i.e. Ku-jen in Chinese). Since he is not going to translate Ko-kaku-ro into the cumbersome "Yellow Crane Tower," he finds Ko-jin goes very musically with Ko-kaku-ro, "Ko-jin goes west from Ko-kaku-ro." Notice how *Ko* in "Ko-jin" goes with the hard *go* in "goes" and with the other K's and O's in Ko-kaku-ro.

The morning rains of Wei Ch'eng moisten the light dust.
(p. 39)

or, as Bynner has it,

A morning-rain has settled the dust in Wei-ch'eng. (p.
191)

is to obstruct the communication of the poem's force.

I cannot, at this point, supply a promising middle between these two approaches in translation, for the problem varies from line to line. Take the line (from "Exile's Letter")

摧 輪 不 道 羊 腸 苦
break/wheel/ not/ say/ sheep/ gut/ hard-going

which alludes to a line in Ts'ao Ts'ao's (A.D. 155-220) "Bitter Cold: A Ballad" which begins

Go north up the T'ai-heng Mountains
How difficult, how steep!
Sheep-Gut Slope so tortuous
Wheels are broken apart

(Translation mine)

Since the line crystallizes the situation of the poem from which the allusion is taken, it can easily be translated without losing its echoes. Pound, in a slightly improvised manner, has captured the essence of this line:

And what with broken wheels and so on, I won't
say it wasn't hard-going
Over roads twisted like sheep's guts.

Many other lines, however, are simply impossible. Pound, determined to abandon annotations, has always tried to get around allusions without deviating from the essential poem.

Lines 13, 14, and 16 from "The Song of Ch'ang-kan" (i.e.
"The River-Merchant's Wife: A Letter") allude respectively to
(1) the story of Wei Sheng who drowned waiting for his
girl who never showed up, (2) to the story of a woman turned
to stone waiting for the return of her husband, and (3)
to perils of sailing by the Yen Yü Rocks as warned by the
boatmen in a popular song: "When the Yen-yü is as big as a
man's hat/ One should not venture to make for Chü-t'ang."[33]
Pound translates these, without annotations, into

13 For ever and for ever and for ever
14 Why should I climb the look out?
15 At sixteen you departed,
16 You went into far Ku-to-yen, by the river
      of swirling eddies

keeping the "faithfulness" or "constancy" in the first story, the
"waiting" in the second, and the "unpassable rapids" in the
third. Naturally we also miss the associations and the subtle
play of

13 If you have the faith of Wei Sheng,
14 Why do I have to climb up the waiting-tower?
                                        (Translation mine)

But between annotations and poetry, one is compelled to make
a choice.

While erudition bothers Pound, so does moralizing. Thus,
the two lines (from the original of "Poem by the Bridge at
Ten-shin") shown on page 143 are removed because, for
Pound not only is the impermanence of man articulated in a
good cluster of images (e.g. flower being driven on the east-

[33] The translation is Waley's. See *The Poet Li Po A.D. 701-762*, p. 19.

功　　成　　身　　不　　退

mission/　done/　body/　not/　retreat

自　　古　　多　　懲一尤

from/　ancient-time/　much/　falling-amiss
(My paraphrase:
Mission accomplished, to stay on
Means, in history, a greater downfall)

flowing waters) but the ending, "he, his own skiffman" already implies the meaning of the two lines in question.[34]

Graphic Ironical Play: Permanence vs Impermanence

In our discussion of "The Beautiful Toilet," we have seen a graphic device Pound employed to emphasize the ironical play of the poem by spacing out one portion of it to play against the other. Any one familiar with Pound's early poetry will remember that most of his imagist poems employ this device. Although the ironical play in these poems is, in a sense, different from the subtle process in the Chinese poem, they all stress an unprepared shift, either to a plane of sense experience entirely different from what goes before it (e.g., "Gentildonna" P, 92) or to a strong contrast (e.g. "The Heather" P, 109). In order to emphasize the interplay of the two planes of differing sensory experience, Pound often spaces them apart (both "Gentildonna" and "The Heather" have this graphic similarity).

This practice is carried over to *Cathay*. As in the case of "The Beautiful Toilet," Pound has, for instance, imposed upon

[34] Pound apparently misunderstood part of the associations, hence the awkward first half of the ending. Compare my approximation and Pound's version.

143

"Leave-Taking Near Shoku" the same kind of graphic structure. In the original, after six lines of quiet exposition of
natural scenery, the narration slips into a different tone. The
lines about life's set courses, from the viewpoint of rhetorical
progress, play an ambiguous role. We do not know if they
are meant to define the meaning of the foregoing scenery or
to become a separate statement. This somewhat nebulous and
noncommittal relation between the two portions becomes, in
Pound's graphic arrangement, not only more emphatic, but
more abrupt. Compare my approximation and Pound's manipulation of this poem:

1 They say the roads to Shu
2 Are too rugged to travel.
3 Mountains rise from the rider's face.
4 Clouds grow along the horse-head.
5 Fragrant trees shroud the plank-paths of Ch'in.
6 Freshets wind the walls of Shu.
7 Ups and downs have set courses.
8 There is no need to ask diviners.

POUND:

1.2 They say the roads of Sanso are steep,
3a Sheer as mountains.
3b The walls rise in a man's face.
4a Clouds grow out of the hill
4b   at his horse bridle.
5a Sweet trees are on the paved way of the Shin,
5b Their trunks burst through the paving,
6a And freshets are bursting their ice
6b   in the midst of Shoku, a proud city.

7 Men's fates are already set,
8 There is no need of asking diviners.

Apparently, Pound is still thinking of the beauty achieved by
having "diverse planes overlie in a certain manner" and wants

144

to manipulate every chance to make the noncommittal relation more perspicuous, just as he makes the ironical play in "The Beautiful Toilet" more striking.

But what concerns us in this section is the way Pound works this graphic principle into the verse line, resulting in the breakup of the line units. Before we turn to examples of this kind in his treatment of some of the Chinese poems, it is important for us to look at a kind of "visual perspicuity" achieved in his early poems by the same graphic principle. Take these lines from "The Coming of War: Actaeon":

> Gray cliffs
>   and beneath them
> A sea
> Harsher than granite.

P, 107

Donald Davie, talking about "Provincia Deserta" (written later than this poem, but earlier than *Cathay*), has come to a conclusion that also explains the above passage: "Pound's lineation points up the distinction of each image or action as it occurs."[35]

This graphic arrangement of the verse line creeps into Pound the translator of Chinese. See how these lines are energized by his rearrangement (my approximation, each line representing one line in the original):

> 5   A Taoist immortal waits for a yellow crane to
>   take flight.
> 6   A seafarer, willy-nilly, follows the white gulls.
> 7   Ch'ü Yüan's songs hang with the sun and moon.
> 8   King Ch'u's terraces are all barren hills now.
>
>   . . . .
>
> 11 If name and rank could last forever,
> 12 The Han river would be northwestward bound.

[35] Davie, p. 62.

145

POUND:

5a Yet Sennin needs
5b/6a A yellow stork for a charger, and all seamen
6b Would follow the white gulls or ride them.
7a Kutsu's prose song
7b Hangs with the sun and moon.

8a King So's terraced palace
8b   is now but barren hill.

. . . .

11 (If glory could last forever
12 Then the waters of Han would flow northward)
From "The River Song"

Pound called a "sennin" an "air spirit" (*Letters*, 180), which is not correct, but "the Taoist immortal" is believed to have "acquired" some sort of supernatural power. As such, the irony within the line is obvious. But Pound, letting the second image assume an equally distinctive position as the first image, "sharpens" the irony. Pound allows two images, like two actors, to *act out* the irony rather than subject themselves to a statement. The graphic rearrangement is a direct confrontation. A few lines later, we find the "barren hill" posing itself menacingly against "King So's terraced palace" with the same dramatic irony. This image of impermanence is preceded by an image of permanence spaced apart from the former. The graphic distance enforces their contrast, between the flight up to the sun and moon and the dissolution into earth, between the immaterial and the material.

A similar rearrangement occurs in these lines from the original of "The City of Choan":

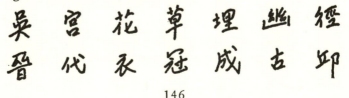

3 Wu/ Palace/ flower/ grass/ bury/ dark
   (secluded)/ path
4 Chin/ Dynasty/ Robes/ Caps/ become/ old/ mound[36]

Two lines, in parallel structure, state one idea: the impermanence of material glory. The stress is upon vicissitude: robes and caps (officials of high-ranking positions) now turned to earth, the secluded path of Wu Palace overgrown with weeds. Pound changes the two-line idea into five lines:

3a Flower and grass
3b Cover over the dark path
3c   where lay the dynastic house of Go.
4a The bright cloths and bright caps of Shin
4b Are now the base of old hills.

The first statement is broken up into different shots; they become so because the images attain greater visuality made possible by graphic arrangement the way a spotlight works. The swift movement from shot to shot—with darkness succeeding brightness ("flower"), dead calm succeeding activity ("cover," which is, in itself, a process of turning light into dark); and stiffness ("lay the dynastic house of Go") succeeding growth ("flower and grass")—necessarily alters the character of the original statement, although the fundamental idea of permanence versus impermanence is the same.[37]

[36] Fenollosa's notes on these lines are not available.

[37] Quite unexpectedly, Pound did not translate the preceding cinematic line in the fashion we would expect. The line is

鳳去臺空江自流

Phoenix gone, terrace empty, river flows on alone.
  (Shot 1)   (Shot 2)   (Shot 3)
Instead of
    Phoenix gone
            terrace empty
                       river flows on alone
Pound gives us
    The phoenix are gone, the river flows on alone.

147

This kind of ironical play "pointed up" by the graphic manipulation of the line is obviously connected with Pound's whole
concept of dynamic acting which we have discussed in great detail in Chapter III. He stresses the *moving* and *leaping* faculty of the language. The breaking up of the line into smaller
units and their graphic arrangement here and in the *Cantos*
must be understood, not only as musical bars but as separate
gestures of an actor in a play emphasized by the spotlight.

A "Poundian" Poem

In a loose sense, all the poems in *Cathay* are, to some extent,
Poundian, because the cuts and turns of the mind in the original poems are either overemphasized or modified according to
his own peculiar gestures of expression. But here is one poem
that deviates most drastically from its Chinese origin, and
does so not in literal details but in the mode of representation.
And it has come to what it is by a very strange way indeed.
This is the poem now entitled "The River Song."

This poem has long been regarded as Pound's principal
"howler," since it represents two of Li Po's poems glued together. The middle section that links them together is the title
of the second poem which Pound mistook as part of the text—
another evidence of Pound's ignorance, for the metrical structure of each line easily marks the unmetrical title off from
the text.

The first poem, which ends at "(If glory could last for
ever/ Then the waters of Han would flow northward),"
is a poem about permanence and impermanence, setting up
poetry as the only sign of immortality. The second poem,
which begins at "The eastern wind brings the green color
into the island grasses at Yei-shu . . . ," describes the luxurious
palace and court life and suggests, through the singing orioles
(i.e. Pound's "nightingales"), the courtiers' search for imperial
favor. The setting of the first is the poet drifting on the river;
the second, in and out of the imperial park with the emperor.

The tone of the first is the strong statement of a poet against superficial glory (name and rank); that of the second, a courtier writing ingratiatingly to the emperor. Although both poems are written by Li Po, the first is earnest self-expression while the second is an occasional poem written with a flattery denounced by the poet in the first poem. One has every reason to believe that, drunk as Li Po always was, he could not have written a poem in which to expose simultaneously the less attractive side of himself against his pronounced pride, although, conditioned by a peculiar occasion, he has written the second kind of poem. The problem here is obviously Pound's. Having misread from Fenollosa's manuscript the title of the second poem as part of the text,[38] Pound was faced with the problem of unity: how was he to hang them together meaningfully?

Let us indulge ourselves here in a kind of rearrangement of Pound's poem. Let us first restore the line units of the original (which Pound breaks up for ironical play) and then omit the middle section, replacing it with the title retranslated.[39] Since all the personal pronouns in the poem are the translator's addition to make sensible English units (see the discussion of "Jade Steps' Grievance" toward the end of Chapter II), let us put them in parentheses to show the universality of the situation in the original:

Chanting on the River
(original title)

This boat is of shato-wood, and its gunwales are magnolia,
Musicians with jewelled flutes and with pipes of
    gold fill full the sides in rows,
And (our) wine is rich for a thousand cups.

[38] Hugh Kenner, p. 33. Kenner did not discuss the poem.
[39] For Pound's original line divisions and my approximation, see Appendix II.

(We) carry singing girls, drift with the drifting water,
Yet sennin needs a yellow stork for a charger,
And all (our) seamen would follow the white gulls or
    ride them.
Kutsu's prose song hangs with the sun and moon.
King So's terraced palace is now but barren hill,
But (I) draw pen on this barge, causing the five
    peaks to tremble,
And (I) have joy in these words like the joy of
    blue islands.
(If glory could last forever
Then the waters of Han would flow northward).

*Poems composed at the command of the Emperor
in I-chün Park on the Dragon-Pond as the
willows are in their fresh green and the new
orioles are singing in their thousand ways*
        (original title for the second poem)

The eastern wind brings the green colour into the island
    grasses at Yei-shu,
The purple house and the crimson are full of spring
    softness.
South of the pond the willow-tips are half-blue and
    bluer,
Their cords tangle in mist, against the brocade-like
    palace.
Vine-strings a hundred feet long hang down from carved
    railings,
And high over the willows, the fine birds sing to each
    other, and listen,
Crying—"Kwan, kuan," for the early wind, and the
    feel of it.
The wind bundles itself into a bluish cloud and wanders
    off.

Over a thousand gates, over a thousand doors are the
    sounds of spring singing,
And the emperor is at Ko.
Five clouds hang aloft, bright on the purple sky,
The imperial guards come forth from the golden house
    with their armour a-gleaming.
The Emperor in his jewelled car goes out to inspect his
    flowers,
He goes out to Hori, to look at the wing-flapping storks,
He returns by way of Sei rock, to hear the new nightin-
    gales,
For the gardens at Jo-run are full of new nightingales,
Their sound is mixed in (this) flute, their voice is in
    the twelve pipes (here).

These two poems obviously move in opposite directions. A
few annotations will clarify even more their diametrically
opposed positions. "Blue islands" in the first poem refers to
the fairyland for people who decide to live in seclusion. Jo-run
(i.e. Shang-lin) Gardens in the second poem refer to courting
with the emperor.[40] Ko (i.e. Capital Hao) refers to the capital
of Kings Wen and Wu of Chou Dynasty (i.e. model rulers).
This allusion goes back to the Greater Odes in *The Classic
Anthology* which reads, in Pound's hand,

He divined, to the 9th straw of ten in the casting
That Hao be the capital for his dwelling;
The tortoise confirmed it; Wu brought it to finish,
    Wu, avatar, how!

(p. 160)

But "King So's terraced palace is now but barren hill." The
last statement in the first poem ("If glory could last for
ever/ Then the waters of Han would flow northward") [i.e.

---

[40] In particular, it refers to the court life described in Ssu-ma
Hsiang-ju's (179-117 B.C.) "The Shang-lin Park." See Burton Watson, *Early Chinese Literature* (New York, 1962), pp. 273-84.

in reverse direction or against nature, for all the rivers in China flow from west to east and from north to south], implies a denunciation of the court, while in the other poem the emperor is praised to the skies.

But Pound's improvisation of the second title not only immediately changes the character of the poems, but links them tightly together.

> And I have moped in the Emperor's garden, awaiting
> an order-to-write!
> I looked at the dragon-pond, with its willow-
> coloured water
> Just reflecting the sky's tinge
> And heard the five-score nightingales aimlessly
> singing.

The strong statement of the permanence of art (which is voiced not only by one person but by many—a process of universalization made possible by the absence of personal pronouns in the original) is turned into the monologue of a *persona.* The speaker is assuming the existence of an audience response, for he now uses the past tense in telling an event proving (to the imaginary audience) the impermanence of the search for glory and the *aimlessness* (which is Pound's sheer invention) of the nightingales' singing,[41] and switches into the present tense again when he breaks into the trance of memory of that event. Notice how "these words" in the line "And I have joy in these words/ like the joy of blue islands" makes him recall "And I have moped in the Emperor's garden, awaiting an order-to-write." What is produced in connection with the search for name and rank (i.e. "order-to-write"), like the pursuit of glory itself, will end in aimlessness.

[41] I do not suppose that Pound wants to call up the associations of this bird the way Eliot uses it in "The Waste Land." But using "nightingales" instead of "orioles" certainly adds a tragic tone to the general atmosphere.

Notice now how the aimless singing of the nightingales pre-
pares for the new ending Pound adds to the poem: all their
singing, being a kind of "order-to-write" just as the song the
speaker had once waited to compose, will end in aimlessness.

> Their sound is mixed in *this* flute
> Their voice is in the twelve pipe *here*.
>
> (Italics mine)

The singing of these courtiers is as transitory as the flutes and
pipes in the previous poem. They do not have the permanence
of Kutsu's (i.e. Chü Yüan's) poetry.

Both the theme, the impermanence of the search for name
and rank, and the time and locale, return to the first poem.
In other words, Pound has incorporated the second poem, by
ironical play again, into the framework of the first poem. As
such, the theme in the first poem aided by the emphatic
graphic play (see previous section) attains a perspicuity that
the second poem, the lines of which Pound did not break up,
does not have. The contrast between the external form of the
first part of the poem and that of the second part is meant
also as a contrast between two forms of life, the one being
carefree and sky-reaching, the other being self-enslaving and
stooping. The stork charges in the first poem, those in the park
merely flap their wings; Kutsu's song hangs with the sun and
moon, the nightingales' song is earthbound. I need not point
out that these nuances are not all in Li Po, because he did not
plan to put them together.

But aside from showing these obvious differences in the
progress between the original and Pound's "howler," let us
try to examine the relation of this maltreated poem to the
Cantos.

One of the easily noticeable stylistic aspects in the *Cantos*
is the abrupt shifts from one plane of experience to another.
Earl Miner tries to see this aspect as a development from
Pound's use of the super-pository technique. Hugh Kenner,

noticing the encyclopedic vision of the *Cantos*, has brilliantly glossed for us the word "periplum," enabling us to understand Pound's thought progress: "The word 'periplum,' which occurs continually throughout the *Pisan Cantos* [74-84], is glossed in Canto LIX: 'periplum, not as land looks on map/ but as sea bord seen by man sailing.' Victor Brerad discovered that the geography of the *Odyssey*, grotesque when referred to a map, was minutely accurate according to the Phoenician voyagers' *periploi*. The image of successive discoveries breaking upon the consciousness of the voyager is one of Pound's central themes."[42] It explains also the rhetorical parallel Pound develops in his style, i.e. the illogical and paratactical movement of the poem.

But be they developed from the super-pository technique or from the more sophisticated "periplum," the different planes of sensory experience rely on some form of correspondence between or among them, hidden in the language. Take the last line of Canto XVII: "Sunset like the grasshopper flying." The tempo (in the word "flying") corresponds to the three lines immediately preceding it,

> Thither Borso, when they shot the barbed arrow at him,
> And Carmagnola, between the two columns,
> Sigismundo, after that wreck in Dalmatia.[43]

But the atmosphere in "sunset like the grasshopper" is prepared and built up about thirty lines earlier:

> Stone trees, white and rose-white in the
> darkness,
> Cypress there by the towers,
> Drift under hulls in the night.

[42] Hugh Kenner, *The Poetry of Ezra Pound* (London, 1951), p. 102.
[43] Earl Miner quoted these lines, but did not elaborate on the subtle nuances that have been built up slowly. See *Ezra Pound, A Collection of Critical Essays*, Walter Sutton, ed. (Englewood Cliffs, N.J., 1963), p. 126.

In the gloom the gold
Gathers the light about it.

This is the extension of the technique of inner correspondence in the "Metro" poem in which (it is worth repeating) the word "black" in the second line merges with the word "apparition" in the first. To hide and prepare *leitmotifs* in the course of the *persona's* reverie is a fundamental way of uniting the disparate planes of consciousness in the *Cantos*.

A slightly different kind of progress is found in the *Pisan Cantos*, Pound's version of *A la récherché du temps perdu*. I have deliberately chosen a much discussed passage, because it is typical of its kind in Pound's later Cantos.[44] This passage is from Canto LXXX:

and for that Christmas at Maurie Hewlett's
Going out from Southampton
they passed the car by the dozen
    who would not have shown weight on a scale
      riding, riding
        for Noel the green holly
Noel, Noel, the green holly
A dark night for the holly

That would have been Salisbury plain, and I have
not thought of
    the Lady Anne for this twelve years
      Nor of Le Portel
How tiny the panelled room where they stabbed him
    In her lap, almost, La Stuarda
    Si tuit li dolh ehl planh el marrimen

    for the leopards and broom plants

---

[44] George Dekker, without having read Achilles Fang's dissertation, *Materials for the Studies of Pound's Cantos* (Harvard, 1958), picked out this passage to show his technique of free association. cf. *The Cantos of Ezra Pound* (New York, 1963), pp. 193-4. Fang spent a long chapter on this passage under the title of "The Technique of Free Association."

Tudor indeed is gone and every rose,
Blood-red, blanch-white that in the sunset glows
Cries: "Blood, Blood, Blood!" against the gothic
  stone
Of England, as the Howard or Boleyn knows.

Instead of attempting another exegesis, the one offered by George Dekker will be as good as any other to show the nature of Pound's technique of free association. Let us quote from him the relevant parts:

> That Pound knew Hewlett and visited these places does not, in itself, matter to his reader, except as far as they stand for something he understands or can understand. Whether Pound can expect his reader to have a necessary superficial acquaintance with Hewlett's work is a question which I can't answer; and it may be that the passage is sufficiently clear without that acquaintance. In any case, Pound did know Hewlett and apparently believed that he embodied peculiarly English virtues and that the English past was still alive in him. And what Pound is implying here and throughout the *Pisan Cantos* is that, yes, it matters very much to him that he knew Hewlett and that he took these journeys; for in so far as the English past is alive and meaningful to him, it is so because of these concrete associations, with man and rooms and journeys; with the Christmas holly in which tree spirits took refuge before the Christmas era; with "the leopards and broom plants" which were the heraldic devices of Richard Coeur-de-lion and the Plantagenets, and with a line from Bertran de Born's Planh for the Young English King, Prince Henry Plantagenet.
>
> Then begins the stanza in which Pound recalls the English roses to life, roses which are the counterparts of leopards and broom plants.[45]

[45] Dekker, pp. 193-94. The last stanza in the quotation models on Fitzgerald's *Rubaiyat*. See also Dekker, p. 192.

Both examples we have cited (without purposely twisting them to suit the present purpose) show clearly that Pound seldom allows the *persona's* conversation to move arbitrarily from one plane of experience to another. The *leitmotifs* are always prepared (usually hidden within the language) before the abrupt shift occurs.

And if we should agree that this is the fundamental principle or organization in the *Cantos*, "The River Song" (the "howler") becomes extremely significant in the development of Pound's style. One might argue, as H. H. Witemeyer has implied in his brilliant discussion of Pound's use of tradition, that his early interest in allusion and thematic transformation prepared for the style in the *Cantos*. But none of Pound's early poems in this category breaks into a world of sensory experience (of considerable length) quite like the *Cantos* (although we must admit both these early poems and the *Cantos* are learned poetry).[46] One might argue, like Eliot half a century ago, that "Provincia Deserta" prepared for "The River Song."[47] This might be true only of a portion of the language in both poems. As one can easily see, the shifts in "Provincia Deserta" are all syntactically clear, i.e. the shifts from one scene to the other are paved by phrases like "I have walked into—," "I have seen—," "I have looked back—," "I have gone in—," "I have climbed—," very much like the directional pointers in Eliot's "Burnt Norton":

> Footfalls echo in the memory
> *Down* the passage which we did not take
> *Toward* the door we never opened
> *Into* the rose garden . . .

---

[46] See H. H. Witemeyer, *Ezra Pound's Poetry, 1908-1916* (Princeton dissertation, 1966), pp. 1-35. He has given us three typical poems of this kind, namely, "In Epitaphium Eius," "Scriptor Ignotus," and "Villonard for this Yule."

[47] Eliot, "Ezra Pound: His Metric and Poetry" (1917) in *To Criticize the Critic* (London, 1963), p. 180.

Through the first gate,
Into our first world, shall we follow
The deception of the thrush?[48]

(Italics mine)

The poem that comes closest to the abrupt shifts (i.e. without directional pointers) in the *Cantos* is "The River Song," for although the super-pository technique in the imagist poems stresses an obvious abruptness, it is restricted to one concrete image rather than an extended stretch of sensory experience containing many images.

One can perhaps say that the internal thought-form in the *Cantos* is a conglomeration of several things: (1) a revival of Pound's early use of allusions, (2) the *persona*, (3) super-pository technique, and (4) the style in "The River Song" characterized by a sudden breaking into the trance of memory (or reverie) and by the employment of hidden *leitmotifs* as bridges between two planes of experience rather than that of directional pointers.

Summing Up

Ezra Pound's life has been long, protean, and disturbing, but it should not blind us to his central preoccupation with the artist and his calling. Thus his translations were first landmarks of his poetry and only secondarily representations of alien literatures. The *Cathay* poems in particular were an important link between his early techniques and theories and the strange land of the *Cantos*. For instance, "The River Song" was an important turning point in his stylistic development. Especially important was the step which Pound took in the manipulation of line-units in translating from the Chinese; they showed a definite progress beyond the interplay of two disparate planes of experience (as in the Metro poem) and beyond the visual perspicuity achieved by graphic arrange-

[48] *The Complete Poems and Plays* (New York, 1952), pp. 117-18.

ment (as in "The Coming of War: Actaeon" and "Provincia Deserta").

The same manipulation of line units was carried over to his later poetry. He stresses simultaneity in the line

Surprised. Desert turmoil. Sea sun.

and spotlights or points up images for visual perspicuity and ironical play in the lines

Flower and grass
Cover over the dark path
    where lay the dynastic house of Go.

He worked these innovations into the line structures of the *Cantos*, as a few quotations will show:

Here is an upward hand, trout, submerged by the eels;
    and from the bank, the stiff herbage
the dry nobbled path, saw many known, and unknown,
for an instant;
    submerging,
The face gone, generation.

                                                16/69

The super-imposition of "eels" upon "trout," and upon "hand," enables the poet to break away from the logic of succession and assume a simultaneity that belongs to the spatial relation in pictorial art. This kind of visual effect is even more striking in the following lines:

Beyond, sea, crest seen over dune
Night sea churning shingle,
To the left, the alley of cypress.

                                        A boat came
One man holding her sail, . . .

                                        17/77

The process of giving the objects visual perspicuity is increasingly dramatic. In the first three lines, Pound still employs directional pointers. They read very much like the director's movie-script. "Beyond" and "to the left" can be taken as stage directions; "sea," "crests seen over dune," "the alley of cypress" are the shots. But in the fourth and the fifth lines, he eliminates stage directions and immediate visual pictures rush toward our retina. This spotlighting is prompted by a graphic arrangement which makes it possible for the poet to eliminate directional pointers and intensify dramatic directness.

Readers may notice also that the first line in both passages quoted is quite un-English. Taken out of its context, the line "Beyond, sea, crest seen over dune" reads like the elliptical style of the word-for-word translation of a Chinese line. Compare, for instance,

> Floating clouds (,) wanderer's mood.
>
> Wave hand (,) from here go.
>
> City spring (,) grass trees thick.
> [Spring (in) city: grass (and) trees (grow)
> deep]

(See Chapter I)

Perhaps the influence of the Chinese language on Pound is illusory, but it is sure that after *Cathay*, he moved more and more toward the paratactical structure and toward the elimination of grammatical links, to achieve the cinematic effects of montage (simultaneity) and spotlight activity. We find, for instance, many such paratactical lines in Canto 49 (which is obviously constructed out of scraps of Chinese poetry):

> Rain; empty river; a voyage
>
> Autumn moon; hills rise above lakes
>
> Broad water; geese line out with the autumn.

(See also Chapter I)

Pound's obsession with simultaneity and visual perspicuity led to his excited explanation of the structure of the Chinese character. The Fenollosa-Pound interpretation of the Chinese ideogram has angered and baffled many readers, because it is faulty, unscholarly, and incompatible with the traditional understanding of the Chinese character. Many sinologists have pointed out the ridiculous extremes to which the Fenollosa-Pound interpretation can lead. I need not repeat their indictment here. But if they were to look at the problem in terms of Pound's own obsessions, they would have made a more unbiased accusation.[49]

The fact is that even if the Pound-Fenollosa explanation of the ideogram were correct, as for instance in the case of *east* (東) and *dawn* (旦), there is no way for the English language to reproduce them *literally* or *physically*. For if we try to reproduce the Chinese character 東 (sun behind tree or, as Pound has it, "sun rising, showing through tree's branches,") we cannot write the word "sun" (日) literally on top of the word "tree," (木) for one word will be crossed out by the other, whereas the Chinese character for sun (日) on top of the character for tree (木) easily forms a new Chinese character, *east* (東). In the case of the Chinese character for dawn (旦) (Pound's "sun above line of horizon,") we cannot reproduce it merely by writing:

SUN
HORIZON

This arrangement is still different from the Chinese 旦 which comes from the pictorial ◯. Any English reproduction of the elements in the two characters will involve the insertion of logical, directional links. Hence, the simultaneous presence

[49] For a good summary of the issue of Pound's ideogrammic method, see William McNaughton, "Ezra Pound et la littérature chinoise" in *Ezra Pound* (L'Herne Edition, Paris, 1965), pp. 509-12. This article also treats, from a different angle, certain points that supplement my view.

of "sun" and "tree" in one picture is rendered into "sun *behind* tree" or "sun *rising, showing* through tree's branches." The insertion of logical, directional links between the objects immediately destroys the simultaneity of the elements in the Chinese characters and allows them to fall back upon the logic of succession. Why, then, was Pound so excited over the structure of the Chinese character?

The answer is that the peculiar qualities of the Chinese character (as it was understood by Pound) sum up the goals he was trying to attain in his poetry, namely, simultaneity, montage, and visual perspicuity. That is why he considered Fenollosa's essay a piece of poetics rather than a treatise on the Chinese character. Pound seemed to be well aware of the fact that directional links or pointers in the English language necessarily destroyed his goal toward simultaneity, for we find many examples in which he tried deliberately to take away the "links" to achieve his purpose:

> Sea sun.   *(Cathay)*

> Green, black, December. Said Mr. Blodgett:
> "Sewing machines will never come into general
>   use . . .
>
>   38/40

> Rain; empty river; a voyage.
>
>   49/38

> Prayer: hands uplifted
> Solitude: a person, a Nurse
> plumes: is she angel or bird, is she a bird
>   or an angel?
>
>   54/101

> Moon,   cloud,   tower,   a patch of the
>   battistero
>   all of whiteness.
>
>   79/62

These are examples of elimination of "links" within the line. But as we have already seen in the previous section, the same technique is worked into the entire skeleton of the *Cantos*. Pound has eliminated many connections between paragraphs to allow impressions to heap and overlie, in quick succession, upon the screen of the readers' imagination, breaking away from the sense of time sequence (as defined and restricted by syntax) to reach for spatial feeling.

Cathay CONSISTS OF only nineteen poems. Many people have translated at least five times as many from the Chinese; but none among these has assumed so interesting and unique a position as *Cathay* in the history of English translations of Chinese poetry and, to some extent, in the history of modern English poetry. For instance, the *vers libre* in *Cathay* prepared the language for later translators. Both John Gould Fletcher, a nonspecialist, and A. C. Graham, a strict sinologist, have pointed out this fact. In an essay entitled "The Orient and Contemporary Poetry," Fletcher writes: "And the point about the *Cathay* translations is this: that every succeeding Chinese translator, beginning with Arthur Waley, whose first book appeared in 1918,[50] has, with very few exceptions, essentially followed the metric scheme set up by Pound. This form— ignoring the "rhymes" and the "tones" of the Chinese originals—directly follows the Chinese construction of the phrase and is therefore the most nearly correct vehicle for translating Chinese poetry we have."[51] A. C. Graham's statement is an open tribute: "The art of translating Chinese poetry is a by-product of the Imagist movement, first exhibited in Ezra Pound's *Cathay* (1915), Arthur Waley's *One Hundred and*

---

[50] The recent reprint of Waley's pamphlet *Chinese Poems* (1916) by F. A. Johns, indicates that Waley had tried other methods which he immediately abandoned. Cf. Chapter I, n. 29.

[51] In *The Asian Legacy and American Life*, Arthur Christy, ed. (New York, 1954), pp. 153-54.

Seventy Chinese Poems (1918)."[52] Although Mr. Graham pays an equal tribute to Arthur Waley, it must be pointed out that not only had Waley acknowledged to Fletcher the metrical debt his Chinese translations have owed to Pound's *Cathay*,[53] but, as we have already seen in Chapter III, many of his translations show that he actually took over Pound's diction and sentence structure.

Considered as translation, *Cathay* ought to be viewed as a kind of re-creation. In these pieces, we cannot expect to find reproduction of all the details (associations, local taste, rhetorical interest inhering in the original language). Instead, we find the "essential poems" preserved in luminous details. As such, they are bound to differ from the originals in the sense that certain literal details are either eliminated or violated; local taste is modified or even altered to suit the English audience and certain allusions are suppressed in order to relieve the readers from the burden of footnotes. And yet, in the examples we have examined, the "cuts and turns" of the mind in the originals are largely preserved, although Pound's ignorance of the Chinese language and Fenollosa's crippled texts occasionally led him into blind alleys.

Most importantly, these poems catalyzed Pound's early techniques. They provided a workshop in which he could mature his poetic talent until it was ready for the explosive appearance of the *Cantos*. Perhaps his translation was only a "process of misinterpretation." But the *Cathay* poems led Pound to the devices which became the foundation of the *Cantos* and thus the hallmarks of a major strain in the poetry of this century. Eliot was perhaps right after all when he said: "Translation is valuable by a double power of fertilizing a literature: by importing new elements which may be assimilated, and by

[52] "Introduction" to *Poems from the Late T'ang* (Baltimore, 1965), p. 13. This book, in which Mr. Graham employed much of Pound's language and post-Empsonian critical techniques, is no doubt the best translation of Chinese poetry so far.

[53] Fletcher, p. 164.

restoring the essentials which have been forgotten in traditional literary method. There occurs, in the process, a happy
fusion between the spirit of the original and the mind of the
translator; the result is not exoticism but rejuvenation."[54]

[54] Eliot, "The Noh and the Image," *Egoist*, iv.7 (August 1917),
102. Whether this judgment is true of Pound's rendering of the Noh
plays remains to be studied. In a sense, these words are certainly true
of *Cathay*.

APPENDICES, BIBLIOGRAPHY,
AND INDEXES

Woman's-room	inside	young	· wife	not	known/knew	sorrow
Spring	day	carefully-making	toilet	ascends	green-painted	storied-house
un-forethought	sees	bank's	head	willow		colour
repents	(having told) taught	her husband	seek	princedom.		

It is the custom of the Chinese to present a willow-branch to one starting on a long journey (perhaps as whip for the ride-horse). Now a newly married girl had yet no experience of what sorrow was. On a fine spring day she makes her toilet with care and ascends a green-painted falcon. Without fore-thought her eyes fall on a willow tree. At the yonder bank, from which she had taken a branch and gave to her husband on parting. The willow is green now as it was then, but this husband is not there. She now experiences what sorrow is and repents having instigated her husband to go on a long journey to try his fortune as soldier.

(by Oshorei)

A Poem by Oshorei (Wang Ch'ang-ling) and
translation in Fenollosa's hand

 *appendix one*

From the Fenollosa Notebooks

ALL Fenollosa's notes for the *Cathay* poems are handwritten in the same format as shown in the illustration on page 168: first, the original Chinese line; second, word-for-word glosses, and third, translation or explanation. For the sake of convenience, the Chinese characters are omitted. However, the original Chinese lines can be found in the discussion of these poems in Chapters III and IV. The text for "Song of the Bowmen of Shu," like the "Unmoving Cloud" which I did not reprint here, contains no Chinese characters.

TEXT FOR "SONG OF THE BOWMEN OF SHU"

Reproduced from Lawrence W. Chisolm's *Fenollosa: The Far East and American Culture* (New Haven-London, Yale University Press, 1963), pp. 251-52.[1]

Sai-bi

(At the epoch of the last emperor of the "In" dynasty, there appeared the two powerful barbarian tribes who often invaded the empire, namely: "Kon-i" in the western part, and "Ken-in" in the northern part of China proper. Bunno was the commander in chief of the western princes; he had to dispatch his army to defend against the outsiders under the order of the emperor. In that time he composed this piece, as if he were one of the soldiers, to show his sweet sympathy to them and to soften their grief and pain. As the commander

[1] According to Hugh Kenner, it was Ariga, not Fenollosa, who wrote down this English version. See Kenner, "Ezra Pound and Chinese," *Agenda*, IV (October-November 1965), 38.

169

was so kind, the soldiers were glad to serve in his army. This is one of the chief reasons why the "Shu" [Chou] dynasty arose and Bunno was esteemed as a saint.)

We picked off the "Warabi" (an edible fern) which first
    grow from the earth.
We say to each other, "When will we return to our coun-
    try?" It will be the last of the year.
Here we are far from our home because we have the "ken-
    in" as our enemy.
We have no leisure to sit down comfortably (as we did
    at home) because we have "ken-in" as our enemy.
We pick off the "Warabi" which are soft.
When we say the returning our mind is full of sorrow.
We are very sorrowful. We are hungry and thirsty.
But our defense is not yet settled, so we cannot let
    our friends return to our country and ask how our
    family lives.
We pick off the "Warabi" which have become already rough.
We say to each other, "When will we return to our coun-
    try?" It will be October.
We must be prudent for our affair (which is the order
    of the emperor); we have no leisure to sit down
    comfortably.
Our sorrow is very bitter, but we would not return to
    the country.
What is that blooming flower?
Whose is that chariot? That is our general's.
The horses are hitched already to the chariot; they
    seem to be vigorous.
How dare we repose? We must conquer the enemy even
    three times in a month.
Those four horses are tied; they are very strong.
The generals are on their backs and the soldiers are
    by their sides.

The four horses are well educated; the generals have
the ivory arrows and the quivers that are ornamented
with the skin of fish.
We must be careful every day, because the enemy is very
quick.
Other time when we started the willows were drooping by
spring wind.
But now we come back when it snows.
We go very slowly and we are thirsty and hungry.
Our mind is full of sorrow; who will know our grief?

ODE 167 TRANSLATED BY BERNHARD KARLGREN
From *The Book of Odes* (Stockholm, 1950), pp. 111-12.

1. We gather the *wei* plant, we gather the *wei* plant,
    the *wei* plant is now sprouting; oh, to go home,
    to go home—the year will (then) be growing late;
    that we have no house, no home, is because of the
    Hien-yün; that we have no leisure to kneel or to
    sit at rest, is because of the Hien-yün.

2. We gather the *wei* plant, we gather the *wei* plant,
    the *wei* plant is now soft; oh, to go home, to go
    home—the hearts are grieved; the grieved hearts
    are burning, we are hungry, we are thirsty; our
    keeping guard is not yet (settled:) finished,
    they do not allow us to go home and enquire (about
    our families).

3. We gather the *wei* plant, we gather the *wei* plant,
    the *wei* plant is now hard; oh, to go home, to go
    home—the year will (then) be in the tenth month;
    the service to the king must not be defective, we
    have no leisure to kneel down or rest; the grieved
    hearts are very sore; we marched away but do not
    come (back).

171

4. What is that ampleness? It is the flowers of the *ch'ang-ti* tree; what chariot is that? It is the carriage of the lord; the war chariots are yoked, the four stallions are robust; how dare we settle down and sit still? In one month there are three victories.

5. We have yoked these four stallions, the four stallions are strong; the lord (leans on=) is conveyed by them and the (small men=) common soldiers are (legging them=) following them on foot; the four stallions are orderly; there are ivory bow-ends and fish (-skin) quivers; should we not daily be on our guard? The Hien-yün are very harassing.

6. Long ago, when we marched, the willows were luxuriant; now when we come (back), the falling snow is thick; we travel the road slowly, we are hungry, we are thirsty; our hearts are pained, nobody (knows:) understands our woe.

TEXT FOR "THE BEAUTIFUL TOILET"
Reproduced from Hugh Kenner, "The Invention of China," *Spectrum*, IX.1 (Spring 1967), 22.

Sei[1]	*Sei*	*Ka*	*han*	*So*
blue	blue	river	bank side	grass

utsu	*utsu*	*en*	*chu*	*rin* [u?]
luxuriantly spread the willow	luxuriantly spread the willow	garden	in	willow

[1] The phonetic transcription is Japanese.

172

yei	*yei*	*so*	*jo*	*jo*
fill	fill	storied	on	girl
full	full	house		

in first bloom
   of youth

Ko	*Ko*	*to*	*So*	*yo*
white	white	just	window	door
brilliant	brilliant	face		
luminous	luminous			

Ga	*Ga*	*Ko*	*fun*	*So*
beauty	beauty	red	powder	toilet
of face	of face	(of berri)		

Sen	*Sen*	*Shutsu*	*so*	*Shu*
slender	slender	put forth	white	hand
			blank	
			not dyed	

Seki	*i*	*Sho*	*Ka*	*jo*
in former	was	courtesan	house	girl
times	(did)			

Kon	*i*	*to*	*Shi*	*fu*
now	is	dissipated	son's	wife

To	*Shi*	*Ko*	*fu*	*Ki*
dissipated	son	go away	not	return

Ku	*Sho*	*nan*	*doku*	*shu*
empty	bed	hard	only one	keep
			alone	

TEXT FOR "LAMENT OF THE FRONTIER GUARD"
Printed by permission of Dorothy Pound,
Committee for Ezra Pound

Extract from Fenollosa notes, September 15, 1896,
"with Mr. Hirai"

[1]   savage   barrier gate   [fertile][1]   wind   sand
The barrier gate near the savage lands is fertile
in wind and sand

[2]   a kind of   rough   at length   end   old
reed called
in Japanese
"ogi."
= the shape of
the wind. "a
red wife" [?]
Everything coming to its end and becoming old
as if withered by the wind

[3]   tree   fall   autumn   grass   yellow
The tree leaves fall, and autumn grass is yellow

[4]   climb   high   expect   savage   savage
                                 (western   (northern
                                 barbarian) barbarian)
                                 "armed"   "robbers" a
                                                meaning
The garrison climbing into the turrets look out
towards the barbarians

[5]   rough   castle   vacant   great   wide
The ruined castle stands vacant in the great desert

[1] Note by Kenner: "fertile" is a guess at illegible word.

[6] side   village   not   leave   fence

The villagers which are far from the capital—
i.e. on frontier—have no fences left for them
(fig.): have no defenders.

[7] white   bone   horizontal   thousand   frost

The white bones lie there during a thousand frosts

[8] a mountain   high mt.   cover   tree   grass
     tangle of   very   a poisonous
     crisscrossed   dense   grass:
     valleys   weeds

Ranges choked or covered by high trees and under
grass

[9] borrow   ask who   emulation to   taking things which
     = tem-   point of op-   belong to others by
     porary   pressing   high rank
     ask   those whom
                          he surpasses

I try to ask who is the tyrant

[10] Heaven   angry   poison   might   martial
                (full of   (good
                spirit like meaning)
                wild horse)

Heaven was angry and inspired martial power:
necessary to use strong medicine—inject it

[11] red   rage   our   sage   Emperor
             angry

Our Emperor became red with anger

[12]   tire   teacher   matter   hi   ko
       to soothe   general of   = becomes   a kind of   ordinary
       the tired   the army   the matter, drum   drum
                                is done   beaten on
                                             horseback
                                             = a certain
                                             kind of music

To soothe the army it became a main matter of
the Emperor to employ music

[13]   positive   mild   change   kill   gas,
       outside   miasma
       (= yo, prin-
       ciple of
       spring)

The mild clear principle turned a poisonous vapor
(denotes the state of the people at the coming
battle)

[14]   let out   soldiers   stir   middle   earth
                                 ("horse" &
                                 "flame" in
                                 character)

Swarming of soldiers irritated to motion the whole state

[15]   three   ten   six   ten   men
                                            thousand
       360,000

[16]   sorry   sorry   tears   like   rain
       (same letter)

Who was sorry? Mr. H. thinks the soldiers. I think it
must have been the families and people

[17]   also   sorrowed   follow   go   serve
       Were sad at having to go to service

176

[18] how   may   work   farmer   farm
How could the farmer work the farm?

[19] not   see   to make an   defend   child
                        expedition,
                        attack
They who go on the expedition of defense will
not come back to see their children

[20] how   know   Kwan   gan   pain
                          barrier gate
How could one know the pain of the soldiers

[21] Ri   Boku   now   not   is
(name of person)
Governor Ri died in unsuccessful attempt to
appease the barbarians

[22] side   men   feed   wolf   tiger
Frontiersmen feed the wolves and tigers
[This is an incident that happened in Go just
before Rihaku. It was in the northwest of China.]

TEXT FOR "SOUTH-FOLK IN COLD COUNTRY"[1]
Reproduced from *Spectrum*, IX.1 (Spring 1967), 50-51.

Another
old style

Dai   horse   not   think   Etsu
The horse of Dai does not think (much of) Etsu

Etsu   bird   not   love   swallow
The bird of Etsu does not love swallow

---

[1] Fenollosa took these notes under the instruction of a Mr. Hirai.

(Dai is a place famous for horses
Etsu is a place famous for certain kind of birds)

feeling   character is   place   learn
Each feeling and character (of a thing) depends upon
the place of its custom

earth   wind   originally   that   like
Air of earth (i.e. local habit) is originally [illegible]
like that

old   separate   wild geese   gate   barrier
In former times I came away from Gammon-barrier

now   defend   dragon   yard   front
           watch
Now I defend in front of dragon yard [2 words illegible]

surprise   sands   mix   sea   sun
This sand surprised confuses the sun rising out of the sea

fly   snow   wander   savage   heavens
The flying snow goes wandering over the wild sky

lice   lice   grow   tiger   bird
young lice   old lice

Vermin grow over the tiger fur and bird feathers (of
the warriors' trappings)

mind   soul   drive   flag   flag (pennons)
Mind and spirit drive on after the battle pennons

pain   battle   merit   not   reward
Merit in the cruel fight gets no reward

loyalty   sincerity   difficult to express
                        are hard to be proved by words
                        can hardly

who   pity   Ri   Hi   general

Who has pity for the Generals Ri and Hi
    they belonged to time of Kan?

White head takes in three sides
who till their old age they were trying to subjugate
the three frontiers

appendix two

Cathay Retranslated

THESE translations are not meant to be a challenge to Pound's nor to any other translator's versions. They are produced here only to show the line-unit and general format of the poems. Where Pound is correct, I do not hesitate to use his words. I have tried to keep my translations both literal and readable for the sake of comparison. To make them into "poetic" translations, I might have to strike off or change a few things. I have numbered each line both in Pound's version and in mine. My version appears on the lefthand page facing Pound's. The following signs need explanation:

(6)   = line or lines not found in the original, being, in most cases, Pound's own invention or deliberate change for certain artistic reasons

1.2   = Two lines in the original are contracted into one by Pound

3a
3b } = One line in the original is broken up
3c   into three lines or line-units by Pound

Pick Ferns, Pick Ferns
from
The Classic Anthology

1 Pick ferns, pick ferns,
2 Ferns are sprouting.
3 Return, return,
4 The year is dusking.
5 No house, no home,
6 The Hsien-yün are the sole cause.
7 No time to rest,
8 The Hsien-yün are the sole cause.

9 Pick ferns, pick ferns,
10 Ferns are soft.
11 Return, return,
12 Hearts are sorrowful.
13 Sorrowful hearts burn, burn.
14 Now hunger, now thirst.
15 Garrison here and there,
16 No message home.

17 Pick ferns, pick ferns,
18 Ferns are coarse.
19 Return, return,
20 The tenth month is here
21 King's affairs still undone,
22 No time to rest,
23 And sorrow pierces heart.
24 We go and return not.

1.2	Here we are, picking the first fern-shoots
3.(4)	And saying: When shall we get back to our country?
5.6	Here we are because we have the Ken-nin for our foemen,
7.8	We have no comfort because of these Mongols.
9.10	We grub the soft fern-shoots,
11.12	When anyone says "Return," the others are full of sorrow.
13.14	Sorrowful minds, sorrow is strong, we are hungry and thirsty.
15.16	Our defence is not yet made sure, no one can let his friend return.
17.18	We grub the old fern-stalks.
(19).20	We say: Will we be let to go back in October?
21.22	There is no ease in royal affairs, we have no comfort.
23.24	Our sorrow is bitter, but we would not return to our country.

25 What is blooming?
26 Flowers of the cherry.
27 Whose imposing chariot?
28 The general's.
29 War-chariot is yoked,
30 Four horses so tall.
31 How dare we settle?
32 One month, three battles.

33 Ride the four horses,
34 Four horses martial in gait.
35 The general rides behind.
36 Beside them, lesser men.
37 Four horses, a grand file.
38 Ivory bow-ends, fish-bone arrow-holders
39 How dare we slake?
40 The Hsien-yün are wide awake.

41 When we set out,
42 Willows dangled green.
43 Now I return,
44 Sleets in a mist.
45 We drag along.
46 Now thirst, now hunger.
47 My heart is full of sorrow.
48 Who knows? who will know?

Song of the Bowmen, continued

25.(26)	What flower has come into blossom?
27.28	Whose chariot? The General's.
29.30	Horses, his horses even, are tired. They were strong.
31.32	We have no rest, three battles a month.
(33).(34)	By heaven, his horses are tired.
35.36	The generals are on them, the soldiers are by them.
37.38	The horses are well trained, the generals have ivory arrows and quivers ornamented with fish-skin.
39.40	The enemy is swift, we must be careful.
41.42	When we set out, the willows were drooping with spring,
43.44	We come back in the snow,
45.46	We go slowly, we are hungry and thirsty,
47.48	Our mind is full of sorrow, who will know of our grief?

By BUNNO, reputedly 1100 B.C.

1   Green beyond green, the grass along the river.
2   Leaves on leaves, the willows in the garden.
3   Bloom of bloom, the girl up in the chamber.
4   A ball of brightness at the window-sill.
5   A flash of fairness is her rouged face.
6   Slender, she puts forth a slender white hand.
7   She was a singing-girl before,
8   Now wife of a playboy.
9   The playboy went and never returned.
10 Empty bed! Alone! How hard it is to keep.

ANONYMOUS

[1] This translation intends to bring out a special point of view. Compare the discussion in Chapter IV.

The Beautiful Toilet[1]

1 Blue, blue is the grass about the river
2 And the willows have overfilled the close garden.
3 And within, the mistress, in the midmost of her
   youth,
4 White, white of face, hesitates, passing the door.
6 Slender, she puts forth a slender hand:

7 And she was a courtesan in the old days,
8 And she has married a sot,
9 Who now goes drunkenly out
10 And leaves her too much alone.

By MEI SHENG, 140 B.C.

---

[1] Line 5 becomes the title.

187

The River Song

1 Magnolia oars; a boat of spice-wood.
2 Jade flutes, gold pipes; musicians fill stern and prow.
3 Bottles of fine wine measuring thousands of pecks.
4 With us are girls; we let loose on drifting waves.
5 A Taoist immortal waits for a yellow crane to take flight.
6 A seafarer, willy-nilly, follows the white gulls.
7 Ch'ü Yüan's songs hang with the sun and moon.
8 King Ch'u's terraces are all barren hills now.
9 High-spirited, I hold pen and shake the Five Peaks.
10 Poem done, I laugh and ride above the Blue Coves.
11 If name and rank could last forever,
12 The Han river would be northwestward bound.

By LI PO

*Poem composed at the command of the Emperor
in I-chün Park on the Dragon-Pond as the
willows are in their fresh green and the new
orioles are singing in their thousand ways*[1]

1 East winds have blown the grass green in Ying-chou.
2 Purple halls, red towers: feel the fine spring day.

1   This boat is of shato-wood, and its gunwales
             are cut magnolia,
2a   Musicians with jewelled flutes and with pipes of gold
2b.3a Fill full the sides in rows, and our wine
3b   Is rich for a thousand cups.
4   We carry singing girls, drift with the drifting water,
5a   Yet Sennin needs
5b.6a A yellow stork for a charger, and all our seamen
6b   Would follow the white gulls or ride them.
7a   Kutsu's prose song
7b   Hangs with the sun and moon.

8a   King So's terraced palace
8b   is now but barren hill,
9a   But I draw pen on this barge
9b   Causing the five peaks to tremble,
10a   And I have joy in these words
10b   like the joy of blue islands.
11   (If glory could last for ever
12   Then the waters of Han would flow northward.)

(Title of next poem)
        And I have moped in the Emperor's garden,
             awaiting an order-to-write!
        I looked at the dragon-pond, with its willow-
             coloured water
        Just reflecting the sky's tinge,
        And heard the five-score nightingales aim-
             lessly singing.

1   The eastern wind brings the green colour into the
             island grasses at Yei-shu,
2   The purple house and the crimson are full of spring
             softness.

3 South of the pool, willows' color is half-green.
4 Reeling smoke, graceful curls, flap the brocade city.
5 Tassel-branches, a hundred feet, dangle about carved columns.
6 And above, nice birds sing to each other:
7 "Kuan, kuan"—the first to get the feel of spring winds.
8 Spring winds roll themselves into the blue clouds.
9 A thousand doors, a million houses, brim with spring voices.
10 The Emperor is now at Capital Hao.
11 Five Clouds pour rays and brighten the Purple Sky.
12 Insignia issue from the golden palace and turn with the "Sun."
13 The "Sky" turns the jade phaeton around the flowers.
14 He goes first to Penglai to see cranes dance
15 And then returns to Chih-shih to listen to new orioles.
16 The new orioles circle above the Shang-lin Park
17 Longing to plunge into the music and mix with the phoenix-pipes.

By LI PO

---

[1] Relevant allusions are given in the discussion of Pound's version in Chapter IV. The following conventional phrases mean:
Five Clouds = auspicious breath = the
    imperial influences on man and nature
Purple Sky = dwelling of the Celestial Emperor
Sun = Emperor
Sky = Emperor

3 South of the pond the willow-tips are half-blue and bluer,

4 Their cords tangle in mist, against the brocade-like palace.

5 Vine-strings a hundred feet long hang down from carved railings,

6 And high over the willows, the fine birds sing to each other, and listen,

7 Crying—"Kwan, Kuan," for the early wind, and the feel of it.

8 The wind bundles itself into a bluish cloud and wanders off.

9 Over a thousand gates, over a thousand doors are the sounds of spring singing,

10 And the Emperor is at Ko.

11 Five clouds hang aloft, bright on the purple sky,

12 The imperial guards come forth from the golden house with their armour a-gleaming.

13 The Emperor in his jewelled car goes out to inspect his flowers,

14 He goes out to Hori, to look at the wing-flapping storks,

15 He returns by way of Sei rock, to hear the new nightingales,

16 For the gardens at Jo-run are full of new nightingales,

17a Their sound is mixed in this flute,

17b Their voice is in the twelve pipes here.

By Rihaku, 8th century A.D.

The Song of Ch'ang-kan

1 My hair barely covered my forehead.
2 I played in front of the gate, plucking flowers,
3 You came riding on a bamboo-horse
4 And around the bed we played with green plums.
5 We were then living in Ch'ang-kan.
6 Two small people, no hate nor suspicion.
7 At fourteen, I became your wife.
8 I seldom laughed, being bashful.
9 I lowered my head toward the dark wall.
10 Called to, a thousand times, I never looked back.
11 At fifteen, I began to perk up.
12 We wished to stay together like dust and ash.
13 If you have the faith of Wei-sheng.[1]
14 Why do I have to climb up the waiting tower?
15 At sixteen, you went on a long journey
16 By the Yen-yü rocks at Ch'ü-t'ang
17 The unpassable rapids in the fifth month
18 When monkeys cried against the sky.
19 Before the door your footprints
20 Are all moss-grown
21 Moss too deep to sweep away.
22 Falling leaves: autumn winds are early.

---

[1] Wei-sheng had a date with a girl at a pillar under the bridge. The girl did not show up. The water came. He died holding tight to the pillar. (From *Shih Chi.*)

The waiting tower in the next line, literally, is wait-for-husband tower or rock which alludes to a story of a woman waiting for the return of her husband on a hill. One version has it that she was turned into a rock while waiting.

The River-Merchant's Wife: A Letter

1 While my hair was still cut straight across my forehead
2 I played about the front gate, pulling flowers.
3 You came by on bamboo stilts, playing horse,
4 You walked about my seat, playing with blue plums.
5 And we went on living in the village of Chokan:
6 Two small people, without dislike or suspicion.

7 At fourteen I married My Lord you.
8 I never laughed, being bashful.
9 Lowering my head, I looked at the wall.
10 Called to, a thousand times, I never looked back.
11 At fifteen I stopped scowling,
12 I desired my dust to be mingled with yours
13 For ever and for ever and for ever.
14 Why should I climb the look out?

15 At sixteen you departed,
16 You went into far Ku-to-yen, by the river of
    swirling eddies,
17 And you have been gone five months.
18 The monkeys make sorrowful noise overhead.

19 You dragged your feet when you went out.
20 By the gate now, the moss is grown, the different
    mosses,
21 Too deep to clear them away!
22 The leaves fall early this autumn, in wind.

23 In the eighth month, butterflies come
24 In pairs over the grass in the West Garden.
25 These smite my heart.
26 I sit down worrying and youth passes away.
27 When eventually you would come down from the Three
     Gorges.
28 Please let me know ahead of time.
29 I will meet you, no matter how far,
30 Even all the way to Long Wind Sand.

By Li Po

23 The paired butterflies are already yellow with August
24 Over the grass in the West garden;
25.26 They hurt me. I grow older.
27 If you are coming down through the narrows of the
river Kiang,
28 Please let me know beforehand,
29 And I will come out to meet you
30   As far as Cho-fu-Sa.

By RIHAKU

Ku Feng No. 18
(After the Style of Ancient Poems)

1 The third month in T'ientsin:
2 A thousand gates of peach and plum trees;
3 In the morning, heart-smiting flowers.
4 In the evening, they drift with eastward water.
5 Water gone and water coming on,
6 Flow, flow from ancient days till now.
7 Today's men are not those of yesterday.
8 Year after year they hang around on the bridge.
9 Cocks crow. Sea sheen stirs.
10 At levee, princes spread in order.
11 The moon falls beyond West Shang-yang Palace.
12 Receding light catches half the wall-towers.
13 Robes and caps shine against the cloud and sun.
14 Levee over, they disperse from the Capital.
15 Saddled horses are like flying dragons,
16 Gold trappings over their heads.
17 Street-people flee in all directions:
18 Haughty indeed, these men's will across the highest peak.
19 Enter doors. Ascend imposing halls.
20 Caldrons with mixed rare food spread out.
21 Fragrant winds usher in the dancing.
22 Clear pipes follow spirited singing.
23 Seventy purple ducks and drakes,
24 Pair by pair, play in the dark of the court,
25 Strive to make merry day and night,

Poem by the Bridge at Ten-Shin

1	March has come to the bridge-head,
2	Peach boughs and apricot boughs hang over a thousand gates,
3	At morning there are flowers to cut the heart,
4	And evening drives them on the eastward-flowing waters.
5	Petals are on the gone waters and on the going,
(6)	And on the back-swirling eddies,
7	But to-day's men are not the men of the old days,
8	Though they hang in the same way over the bridge-rail.
9	The sea's colour moves at the dawn
10	And the princes still stand in rows, about the throne,
11	And the moon falls over the portals of Sei-go-yo,
12	And clings to the walls and the gate-top.
13	With head gear glittering against the cloud and sun,
14	The lords go forth from the court, and into far borders.
15	They ride upon dragon-like horses,
16	Upon horses with head-trappings of yellow metal,
17	And the streets make way for their passage.
18	Haughty their passing,
19a	Haughty their steps as they go in to great banquets,
19b.20	To high halls and curious food,
21	To the perfumed air and girls dancing,
22	To clear flutes and clear singing;
23	To the dance of the seventy couples;
24	To the mad chase through the gardens.
25	Night and day are given over to pleasure

26 And pass a thousand autumns, they say.
27 Mission accomplished, to stay on
28 Means, in history, a greater downfall.
29 Li Ssu, at death, sighed over his yellow dog.[1]
30 Lady Lü-chu's beauty triggered tragic rivalry.[2]
31 None can compare to Fan-li[3]
32 Who loosened his hair and went a-boating.

By LI Po

[1] Li Ssu, a prime minister in the Ch'in Dynasty, fell from grace and was to be executed in the Capital. On the way he remarked to his son, "I wish I could bring our yellow dog and go rabitting with you again!" At that, they both wept. (From *Shih-chi*).

[2] This line refers to the story of Lü Chu recorded in the biography of Shih Ch'ung (249-300). Lü Chu, Green Pearl, is Shih's most beloved concubine. Sun Hsiu, a high-ranking official, sued for her. Shih refused him. Sun made false mandates to execute Shih. "Now I shall be executed on account of you" said Shih to Lü Chu who wept and replied, "It is fit for me to die before you" and jumped down from the top storey to death.

[3] Fan Li, after having succeeded in helping the king of Yüeh to overthrow the king of Wu, retreated from public life.

Poem by the Bridge, continued

26a	And they think it will last a thousand autumns,
(26b)¹	Unwearying autumns.
29	For them the yellow dogs howl portents in vain,
30a	And what are they compared to the lady Riokushu,
30b	That was cause of hate!
31	Who among them is a man like Han-rei
32a	Who departed alone with his mistress,
32b	With her hair unbound, and he his own skiffsman!

By RIHAKU

¹ Lines 27 and 28 are omitted.

199

Yü Chieh Yüan
(Jade Steps' Grievance)

1 Upon the jade steps white dews grow.
2 It is late. Gauze stockings are dabbled.
3 She lets down the crystal blind
4 To watch, glass-clear, the autumn moon.

By LI PO

The Jewel Stairs' Grievance[1]

1 The jewelled steps are already quite white with dew,
2 It is so late that the dew soaks my gauze stockings,
3 And I let down the crystal curtain
4 And watch the moon through the clear autumn.

By RIHAKU

[1] Jewel stairs, therefore a palace. Grievance, therefore there is something to complain of. Gauze stockings, therefore a court lady, not a servant who complains. Clear autumn, therefore he has no excuse on account of weather. Also she has come early, for the dew has not merely whitened the stairs, but has soaked her stockings. The poem is especially prized because she utters no direct reproach.

Ku Feng No. 14

1   The barbarian pass is filled with windblown sand
2   Squalling from ancient times till now.
3   Trees stripped of leaves, autumn grass go yellow.
4   We climb up to look over the barbarous land:
5   Desolate castle, vast empty desert,
6   No wall left to this frontier village,
7   White bones lying across a thousand frosts,
8   Huge mounds, covered by thorns and brushwoods.
9   Who is the aggressor? Let me ask.
10 The barbarians' malicious martial move
11 Has brought the emperor's flaming anger.
12 He ordered the army to beat the war-drums.
13 Calm sun turned into murderous air.
14 He called for soldiers, causing a turmoil over the
       Middle Kingdom.
15 Three hundred and sixty thousand men.
16 Sorrow, sorrow, tears like rain.
17 Grief-drenched, yet we had to go.
18 How are we to farm our fields?
19 Without seeing the frontier men
20 Who would know the dreary sorrow at the pass?
21 General Li Mu is no longer here.
22 We guardsmen fed to tigers and wolves.

By Li Po

Lament of the Frontier Guard

1   By the North Gate, the wind blows full of sand,
2   Lonely from the beginning of time until now!
3   Trees fall, the grass goes yellow with autumn.
4a I climb the towers and towers
4b   to watch out the barbarous land:
5   Desolate castle, the sky, the wide desert.
6   There is no wall left to this village.
7   Bones white with a thousand frosts,
8   High heaps, covered with trees and grass;
9   Who brought this to pass?
11 Who has brought the flaming imperial anger?
12 Who has brought the army with drums and with
     kettle-drums?
10 Barbarous kings.
13 A gracious spring, turned to blood-ravenous autumn,
14 A turmoil of wars-men, spread over the middle
     kingdom,
15 Three hundred and sixty thousand,
16 And sorrow sorrow like rain.
17 Sorrow to go, and sorrow, sorrow returning.
18 Desolate, desolate fields,
19 And no children of warfare upon them,
19a   No longer the men for offence and defence.
20 Ah, how shall you know the dreary sorrow at the
     North Gate,
21 With Rihoku's name forgotten,
22 And we guardsmen fed to the tigers.

By RIHAKU

Remembering Our Excursion in the Past:
A Letter Sent to
Commissary Yen of Ch'ao County.

1 I remembered Tung Tsao-chiu of Lo-yang
2 Who once built me a wine-shop south of T'ientsin Bridge.
3 Yellow gold, white jade to buy songs and laughter.
4 Drunk for months on end; in our eyes, no king, no lord.
5 Among cloud-riding worthies and heroes all over the world
6 With you I was most in tune.
7 To us, mountain-crossing and sea-crossing meant nothing,
8 Our hearts and minds were open: nothing to hold back.
9 I went south of Huai River to clamber along laurel boughs.
10 You stayed north of Lo, dreaming, thinking, sad.
11 Wanting no separation,
12 We came together,
13 Together to visit the removed City of Immortals.
14 Thirty-six turns of whirling and winding water.
15 Entering—a stream of a thousand bright flowers.
16 Millions of valleys we passed; surges of pine-winds.
17 Horses with silver saddles and gold trappings arrived at level ground.
18 The magistrate of East Han came to meet us.
19 The "True Man" of Tzu-yang

(0)   To So-Kin of Rakuyo, ancient friend, Chancellor of
      Gen.

1   Now I remember that you built me a special tavern

2   By the south side of the bridge at Ten-Shin.

3   With yellow gold and white jewels, we paid for
      songs and laughter

4   And we were drunk for month on month, forget-
      ting the kings and princes.

5   Intelligent men came drifting in from the sea and
      from the west border,

6a   And with them, and with you especially,

6b   There was nothing at cross purpose,

7a   And they made nothing of sea-crossing or of
      mountain-crossing,

(7b) If only they could be of that fellowship,

8   And we all spoke out our hearts and minds, and
      without regret.

9a   And then I was sent off to South Wei,

9b   smothered in laurel groves,

10a   And you to the north of Raku-hoku

10b   Till we had nothing but thoughts and memories
      in common.

11   And then, when separation had come to its worst,

12.13 We met, and travelled into Sen-Go,

14   Through all the thirty-six folds of the turning and
      twisting waters,

15a   Into a valley of the thousand bright flowers,

(15b) That was the first valley;

16   And into ten thousand valleys full of voices and
      pine-winds.

17   And with silver harness and reins of gold,

18   Out came the East of Kan foreman and his company.

19   And there came also the "True man" of Shi-yo
      to meet me,

20 Invited me to play the jade flute.
21 On the Tower of Feasting Mist celestial music stirred,
22 Blending, echoing like phoenix cries.
23 Long sleeves, touched by the flutes, tended to rise.
24 The magistrate of Middle Han, now drunk, began
    to dance,
25 His hand holding a brocade robe to cover me.
26 Drunk, I wanted to sleep and pillowed on his thigh.
27 At the banquet our spirit soared beyond the nine
    skies,
28 Stars parted, rain scattered before the morning came.
29 Into different directions from Ch'u, over distant
    mountains and rivers.
30 I went back myself to the mountains, my old nest.
31 And you returned home, crossing the Wei Bridge.
32 Your father, brave like a leopard or tiger,
33 Then governor of *Ping* to halt barbarians,
34 Called me in May to cross the T'ai-heng ranges.
35 Broken wheels, I don't have to say, over sheep-gut
    roads
36 And late in the year arrived at Liang in the north,
37 Moved at your weighing friendship over gold.
38 Jade cups, rich dishes on emerald trays
39 Made me drunk, food-full, no more thoughts of
    returning home.
40 Often we went out west of the City to the bend

20	Playing on a jewelled mouth-organ.
21	In the storied houses of San-Ko they gave us more Sennin music,
22	Many instruments, like the sound of young phoenix broods.
23a	The foreman of Kan Chu, drunk, danced
23b	because his long sleeves wouldn't keep still
24	With that music playing
25.26	And I, wrapped in brocade, went to sleep with my head on his lap,
27	And my spirit so high it was all over the heavens,
28	And before the end of the day we were scattered like stars, or rain.
29	I had to be off to So, far away over the waters,
(30).31	You back to your river-bridge.
32	And your father, who was brave as a leopard,
33	Was governor in Hei Shu, and put down the barbarian rabble,
34a	And one May he had you send for me,
34b	despite the long distance.
35a	And what with broken wheels and so on, I won't say it wasn't hard going.
35b	Over roads twisted like sheeps' guts.
36a	And I was still going, late in the year,
36b	in the cutting wind from the North,
37a	And thinking how little you cared for the cost,
37b	and you caring enough to pay it.
(38a)	And what a reception:
38b	Red jade cups, food well set on a blue jewelled table,
39	And I was drunk, and had no thought of returning.
40	And you would walk out with me to the western corner of the castle,

41 Around the Chin Temple where there was a river
    like green jade.
42 Float a boat; stir the water; flutes and drums joined.
43 A little wave; dragon scales; cyperaceous green.
44 At the impulse, we brought girls and drifted to
    and fro.
45 They were like catkins, or rather, flakes of snow.
46 Rouge makeup, like drunkenness, to go with the
    sunset.
47 On the green water, a hundred feet deep, was written
    the eyebrows.
48 Green eyebrows, fair and refined; bright, crescent-
    bright.
49 Beautiful girls sang in turn, as the brocade swirled
    into dance.
50 Clear winds blew the songs into the sky,
51 And the songs flew around the clouds.
52 Such a moment, such pleasure, was difficult to have
    again.
53 I went west to offer "Rhymeprose on the Long Willow"
54 Blue-cloud fame in the court was unattained.
55 To East Ranges, white-headed, I returned
56 And met you again south of Bridge of Wei.
57 North of Chan, we made separation.

41   To the dynastic temple, with water about it clear
as blue jade,

42   With boats floating, and the sound of mouth-organs
and drums,

43   With ripples like dragon-scales, going grass-green
on the water,

44   Pleasure lasting, with courtesans, going and coming
without hindrance,

45   With the willow flakes falling like snow,

46   And the vermillioned girls getting drunk about
sunset,

47   And the water, a hundred feet deep, reflecting
green eyebrows

48a   —Eyebrows painted green are a fine sight in young
moonlight,

48b   Gracefully painted—

49a   And the girls singing back at each other,

49b   Dancing in transparent brocade,

50   And the wind lifting the song, and interrupting it,

51   Tossing it up under the clouds.

52a   And all this comes to an end.

52b   And is not again to be met with.

53a   I went up to the court for examination,

53b   Tried Layu's luck, offered the Choyo song,

54   And got no promotion,

55a   and went back to the East Mountains

55b   White-headed.

56   And once again, later, we met at the South bridge-
head.

57   And then the crowd broke up, you went north to
San palace,

58 You asked me how much sadness I know:
59 Falling flowers at spring dusk bustle in confusion.
60 To talk about it? There is no end.
61 To spell my emotion? There is no word.
62 I call my son to kneel down and seal this letter
63 And send it to you, a thousand miles, and thinking.

By Li Po

To See Yüan Erh Off as Envoy to An-hsi

1 Wei City: morning rain soaks the light dust.
2 By the inn, green upon green, willows' color is new.
3 You had better drink one cup more before going!
4 West of Yang Pass, you will have no friends.

By Wang Wei

58   And if you ask how I regret that parting:
59a   It is like the flowers falling at Spring's end
59b   Confused, whirled in a tangle.
60   What is the use of talking, and there is no end of
        talking,
61   There is no end of things in the heart.
62a   I call in the boy,
62b   Have him sit on his knees here
62c   To seal this,
63   And send it a thousand miles, thinking.

By RIHAKU

Four Poems of Departure

1   Light rain is on the light dust.
2a   The willows of the inn-yard
2b   Will be going greener and greener,
3   But you, Sir, had better take wine ere your departure,
4a   For you will have no friends about you
4b   When you come to the gates of Go.

By RIHAKU or OMAKITSU

211

To See Meng Hao-jan Off to Yang-chou

1 My old friend goes away from the Yellow Crane
    Tower.
2 In smoke-flower third month down to Yang-chou.
3 A lone sail, a distant shade, lost in the blue horizon.
4 Only the long Yangtze is seen flowing into the sky.

By LI Po

Taking Leave of a Friend

1 Green mountains lie across the north wall.
2 White water winds the east city.
3 Here once we part,
4 Lone tumbleweed, a million miles to travel.
5 Floating clouds, a wanderer's mood.
6 Setting sun, an old friend's feeling.
7 We wave hands, you go from here.
8 Neigh, neigh, goes the horse at parting.

By LI Po

Separation on the River Kiang

1 Ko-jin goes west from Ko-kaku-ro,
2 The smoke-flowers are blurred over the river.
3 His lone sail blots the far sky.
4a And now I see only the river,
4b   The long Kiang, reaching heaven.

By RIHAKU

Taking Leave of a Friend

1 Blue mountains to the north of the walls,
2 White river winding about them;
3 Here we must make separation
4 And go out through a thousand miles of dead grass.

5 Mind like a floating wide cloud,
6 Sunset like the parting of old acquaintances
7 Who bow over their clasped hands at a distance.
8 Our horses neigh to each other as we are departing.

By RIHAKU

To See a Friend Off to Shu (*Szechuan*)

1 They say the roads to Shu
2 Are too rugged to travel.
3 Mountains rise from the rider's face.
4 Clouds grow along the horse-head.
5 Fragrant trees shroud the plank-paths of Ch'in.
6 Freshets wind the walls of Shu.
7 Ups and downs have set courses.
8 There is no need to ask diviners.

By LI PO

Ascend the Phoenix Terrace in Chin-ling

1 The phoenix were at play on the phoenix terrace.
2 The phoenix are gone, the terrace empty, the river
   flows on alone.
3 Flowers and weeds bury the dark paths of the Wu
   palace.
4 Robes and caps of Chin Dynasty have gone into the
   grave mounds.
5 The Three Mountains half-falling beyond the sky,
6 White Heron Isle splits the river into two.
7 There are always floating clouds covering the sun;
8 Unable to see Ch'ang-an, I am caught in grief.

By LI PO

214

Leave-Taking Near Shoku

"Sanso, King of Shoku, built roads"

1.2 They say the roads of Sanso are steep.
3a Sheer as the mountains.
3b The walls rise in a man's face,
4a Clouds grow out of the hill
4b   at his horse's bridle.
5a Sweet trees are on the paved way of the Shin,
5b Their trunks burst through the paving,
6a And freshets are bursting their ice
6b   in the midst of Shoku, a proud city.

7 Men's fates are already set,
8 There is no need of asking diviners.

By RIHAKU

The City of Choan

1 The phoenix are at play on their terrace.
2 The phoenix are gone, the river flows on alone.
3a Flowers and grass
3b Cover over the dark path
3c   where lay the dynastic house of the Go.
4a The bright cloths and bright caps of Shin
4b Are now the base of old hills.

5 The Three Mountains fall through the far heaven,
6a The isle of White Heron
6b   splits the two streams apart.
7 Now the high clouds cover the sun
8a And I cannot see Choan afar
8b And I am sad.

215

1   North-born horses do not think of Yüeh in the south.
2   Fowls of Yüeh do not love Yen, the north region.
3   Nature and feeling are born of habit.
4   Likewise, native manners.
5   We took leave at the Wild-goose Pass,
6   And are now garrisoned at the Dragon-Court.
7   Startling sand confounds the sun above the "Vast Sea."[1]
8   Flying snow bewilders the barbarian sky.
9   Lice grow inside helmets and mails.
10   Our spirit is driven with the silken banners.
11   Hard fight earns no imperial reward.
12   Royalty is difficult to express.
13   Who would pity the Winged General Li,
14   Who, white-headed, was lost among the border states?[2]

By LI PO

[1] The Vast Sea (*han-hai*) is the ancient name for the Mongolian desert, so named because "the sand flies like waves and people and horses are lost in it as if sinking."
[2] Li Kuang, died 125 B.C.

216

South-Folk in Cold Country

(1) The Dai horse neighs against the bleak wind of
    Etsu,

2 The birds of Etsu have no love for En, in the
    North,

3.4 Emotion is born out of habit.

5 Yesterday we went out of the Wild-Goose gate,

6 To-day from the Dragon-Pen.[1]

7 Surprised. Desert turmoil. Sea sun.

8 Flying snow bewilders the barbarian heaven.

9 Lice swarm like ants over our accoutrements.

10 Mind and spirit drive on the feathery banners.

11 Hard fight gets no reward.

12 Loyalty is hard to explain.

13a Who will be sorry for General Rishogu,

13b   the swift moving,

14 Whose white head is lost for this province?

---

[1] I.e., we have been warring from one end of the empire to the other, now east, now west, on each border.

1   Kingfishers sport among orchids and begonias,
2   Color to color, sheen flashes upon sheen.
3   Green vines braid into the high forest.
4   Thick foliage roofs a whole mountain.
5   Beneath these a lone meditative man
6   Silently whistles, plucking at the clear strings.
7   He lets loose his heart through the sky,
8   Chews pistils and bails out flying fountains.
9   The "Red Pine" stands before the up-stream,[1]
10 Riding a wild-goose upon the purple smoke.
11 He takes "Floating Hill" by the sleeve
12 And pats the "Vast Cliff" upon the shoulder.
13 You, you ephemeras
14 Would you rather know the age of a turtle?

By KUO P'U

---

[1] Red Pine, Floating Hill, Vast Cliff are the names of three famous Taoist elites. The names themselves show the stress of the Taoist metaphysics on the desire to become consonant with nature.

Sennin Poem by Kakuhaku

1a The red and green kingfishers
1b   flash between the orchids and clover,
2   One bird casts its gleam on another.

3   Green vines hang through the high forest,
4   They weave a whole roof to the mountain,
5   The lone man sits with shut speech,
6   He purrs and pats the clear strings.
7   He throws his heart up through the sky,
8a He bites through the flower pistil
8b   and brings up a fine fountain.
9   The red-pine-tree god looks at him and wonders.
10 He rides through the purple smoke to visit the
        sennin,
11 He takes "Floating Hill"[1] by the sleeve,
12 He claps his hand on the back of the great water
        sennin.

13 But you, you dam'd crowd of gnats,
14 Can you even tell the age of a turtle?

---

[1] Name of a sennin.

Ballad of the Mulberry Road

I

1 The sun rises in the southeast corner,
2 Shining upon the chambers of our Ch'ins.
3 In them a pretty girl
4 Self-named Lo-fu.
5 Lo-fu loves silkworms and mulberry-trees.
6 She plucks leaves south of the walls.
7 Green silk for her basket-trappings.
8 Cassia-bough for her basket-handle.
9 On her head, a dangling plait,
10 At her ears, bright moon pearls.
11 Yellow satin for her skirt beneath.
12 Purple satin for her short-coat above.
13 Passers-by seeing Lo-fu
14 Put down their loads to twirl their moustaches
   and beard.
15 Young men seeing Lo-fu
16 Take off their hats to re-do their head-dresses.
17 Farmers forgot their ploughs.
18 Hoemen forgot their hoes.
19 When they get home they are all irritated
20 After having watched Lady Lo-fu.

II

21 From the south comes the Prefect,
22 His five horses falter their pace.
23 The Prefect sends an officer over
24 To ask whose daughter she can be.

Ballad of the Mulberry Road

1   The sun rises in south-east corner of things

2   To look on the tall house of the Shin

3   For they have a daughter named Rafu (pretty girl),

4   She made the name for herself: "Gauze Veil,"

5   For she feeds mulberries to silkworms,

6   She gets them by the south wall of the town.

7   With green strings she makes the warp of her basket,

8a She makes the shoulder-straps of her basket

8b   from the boughs of Katsura,

9   And she piles her hair up on the left side of her head-piece.

10   Her earrings are made of pearl,

11   Her underskirt is of green pattern-silk,

12   Her overskirt is the same silk dyed in purple,

13   And when men going by look on Rafu

14a   They set down their burdens,

14b They stand and twirl their moustaches.

                       (FENOLLOSA MSS., very early)

25 "In the chambers of Ch'in the pretty girl
26 Self-named Lo-fu."
27 "How old, tell me, is this Lo-fu?"
28 "Not quite twenty
29 But well past her teens."
30 The Prefect sends words to Lo-fu:
31 "Would you ride together with me?"
32 Lo-fu walks up and to him says:
33 "How unthinking you are!
34 Just as you have your wife,
35 I, too, have my husband."

III

36 "From the east, a thousand horses.
37 My husband rides at the head.
38 How to tell my husband?
39 White steed followed by black colt,
40 Green silk hangs from its tail,
41 Gold trappings upon its head.
42 At his waist, a windlass sword
43 Worthy of million pieces of gold.
44 At fifteen, he became a page.
45 At twenty, he attended court.
46 At thirty, among the emperor's council,
47 At forty, assigned to govern a city,
48 He is a man, clean and white
49 With a little beard.
50 Stately, he walks to the Prefecture.
51 Proudly, he steps back and forth.
52 Seated there, several thousand men.
53 All say my husband the finest of all."

ANONYMOUS

The Old Idea of Ch'ang-an
(part)[1]

1   Ch'ang-an's thoroughfare leads into narrow, side lanes,
2   Dark oxen, white horses, seven scented coaches.
3   Jade phaeton goes freely past the regal house.
4   Gold whips,[2] like unbroken silk, wave toward
     barons' homes.
5   Canopy, as if mouthed by a dragon, holds the
     morning sun.
6   Tassels, as if spat out by a phoenix, brings the afterglow.
7   Hundred feet of gossamer strive to enfold trees.
8   A flight of graceful birds sing to the flowers.
9   Sung to, flowers and sporting butterflies by a thousand
     gates.
10 Jade-trees, silver-terraces, a myriad of colors.

[1] The original poem is 68 lines. Pound translated only the first
sixteen lines.
[2] Gold whips are a synecdoche for horses.

Old Idea of Choan by Rosoriu

I

1   The narrow streets cut into the wide highway
     at Choan,
2a   Dark oxen, white horses,
2b   drag on the seven coaches with outriders
2c   The coaches are perfumed wood,
3a   The jewelled chair is held up at the crossway,
3b   Before the royal lodge:
4a   A glitter of golden saddles, awaiting the princess;
4b   They eddy before the gate of the barons.
5a   The canopy embroidered with dragons
5b   drinks in and casts back the sun.
6a   Evening comes.
6b   The trappings are bordered with mist.
7a   The hundred cords of mist are spread through
7b   and double the trees,
8a   Night birds, and night women,
8b   Spread out their sounds through the gardens.

II

9a   Birds with flowery wing, hovering butterflies
9b   crowd over the thousand gates.
10a   Trees that glitter like jade,
10b   terraces tinged with silver,
10c   The seed of a myriad hues,

11 Covered ways and interlaced windows form a paired pattern.

12 Double gates and joining eaves hang out phoenix-wings.

13 Painted towers of Liang rise into the middle of the sky.

14 Gold pillars of Emperor Han go straight up the clouds.

15 Before the chambers, to look at each other and remain strangers.

16 On the road, how, on earth, can we know each other if met?

By Lu Chao-lin

11   A network of arbours and passages and covered
          ways,
12a Double towers, winged roofs,
12b   border the network of ways:
(12c) A place of felicitous meeting.
13a Riu's house stands out on the sky,
13b   with glitter of colour
14a As Butei of Kan had made the high golden lotus
14b   to gather his dews,
15   Before it another house which I do not know:
16a How shall we know all the friends
16b   whom we meet on strange roadways?

Still Clouds
with introduction

Still clouds; thoughts of friends and relatives. A full bottle
of fresh wine; the garden stretches its new luxuriance. Day in,
day out, no prospects; it is hard to repress my swelling lapel.

I

1 Tier upon tier—the still clouds.
2 Mist over mist—the seasonal rains.
3 All Eight Directions are darkened.
4 All flat roads are blocked.
5 I stay speechless in the east chamber,
6 And alone pat a bottle of spring wine.
7 Good friends are away in the blurring distance.
8 I scratch my head and stand still.

II

9   The still clouds—tier upon tier.
10 The seasonal rains—mist over mist.
11 All Eight Directions are darkened.
12 All flat land is turned river.
13 Wine is here, here is wine.
14 At leisure, I drink by the east window.
15 Day in, day out, thoughts of friends.
16 And no boat, no carriage, approaches.

To-Em-Mei's "The Unmoving Cloud"

"Wet Springtime," says
To-Em-Mei, "Wet Spring in the Garden."

I

1	The clouds have gathered, and gathered,
2	and the rain falls and falls,
3a	The eight ply of the heavens
3b	are all folded into one darkness,
4	And the wide, flat road stretches out.
5	I stop in my room toward the East, quiet, quiet,
6	I pat my new cask of wine.
7	My friends are estranged, or far distant,
8	I bow my head and stand still.

II

9.10	Rain, rain, and the clouds have gathered,
11	The eight ply of the heavens are darkness,
12	The flat land is turned into river.
13	'Wine, wine, here is wine!'
14	I drink by my eastern window.
15	I think of talking and man,
16	And no boat, no carriage, approaches.

III

17 The trees in the east garden
18 Heavy with leafy boughs
19 Strive in their fresh fashion
20 To invite my attention.
21 Men also have their say
22 As sun and moon on their trek.
23 How to get friends to sit close by
24 To talk about past and present?

IV

25 Wing to wing, the birds fly,
26 Perch to rest in my courtyard tree,
27 Close their wings at ease
28 And in good voice echo each other in unison:
29 "Not that there is no one around
30 But that I think of you more."
31 Day in, day out, no response.
32 How sorrowful am I!

By T'ao Ch'ien (365-427)
[T'ao Yüan-ming]

III

17	The trees in my east-looking garden
18	are bursting out with new twigs,
19.20	They try to stir new affection,
21.22	And men say the sun and moon keep on moving
23.(24)	because they can't find a soft seat.
25.26	The birds flutter to rest in my tree,
27.28	and I think I have heard them saying,
29	"It is not that there are no other men
30	But we like this fellow the best,
31	But however we long to speak
32	He cannot know of our sorrow."

By Tao Yuan Ming,
365-427 A.D.

selected bibliography

Primary Sources

BOOKS

A Lume Spento (Venice, 1908).

A Quinzaine for This Yule (London, 1908).

A Lume Spento and Other Early Poems (New Directions, 1965). Reproduces all of the original *A Lume Spento* and *A Quinzaine for This Yule*, and publishes for the first time "Some Poems from the 'San Trovaso' Notebook" written by Pound in Venice in 1908.

Personae (London, 1909).

Exultations (London, 1909).

The Spirit of Romance (London, 1910 and New Directions [1953]).

Provenca (Boston, 1910).

Canzoni (London, 1911).

Ripostes (London, 1912).

Sonnets and Ballate of Guido Cavalcanti (London, 1912).

Des Imagistes, ed. Ezra Pound (New York, 1914).

Cathay (London, 1915).

Gaudier-Brzeska: A Memoir (London, 1916).

Lustra (London, 1916).

Lustra (New York, 1917).

Pavannes and Divisions (New York, 1918).

Quia Pauper Amavi (London, 1919).

Instigations (London, 1920).

Hugh Selwyn Mauberley (London, 1920).

Umbra (London, 1920).

Personae (London, 1926).

Selected Poems (London, 1928).

Profile, ed. Ezra Pound (Milan, 1932).

Active Anthology, ed. Ezra Pound (London, 1933).

ABC of Reading (London, 1934 and New Directions, 1960).
Make It New (London, 1934).
Polite Essays (London, 1937).
Confucius: The Unwobbling Pivot & The Great Digest (New Directions, 1947).
Guide to Kulchur (London, 1938 and New Directions [1953]).
Personae (New Directions [1949]).
The Letters of Ezra Pound (New Directions, 1950).
The Translations of Ezra Pound (New Directions, 1953).
Literary Essays of Ezra Pound, ed. T. S. Eliot (London, 1954).
The Classic Anthology, Defined by Confucius (New York, 1955).
Impact: Essays on Ignorance and the Decline of American Civilization, ed. Noel Stock (Chicago, 1960).
Confucius to Cummings: An Anthology of Poetry, ed. with M. Spann (New York, 1964).
The Cantos of Ezra Pound (London, New Collected Edition, 1965).

ARTICLES

1909

"What I Feel About Walt Whitman," *American Literature*, XXVII (1955).

1911-1912

"I Gather the Limbs of Osiris," *The New Age*, x (November 1911-February 1912). Twelve parts:
1. "A Translation from the Early Anglo-Saxon Text," p. 107, appearance of Pound's *The Seafarer*.
2. "A Rather Dull Introduction," pp. 130-31.
3. "Guido Cavalcanti," pp. 155-56. Includes translations.
4. "A Beginning," pp. 178-80.
5. "Four Early Poems of Arnaut Daniel," pp. 201-02. Verse translations.

234

SELECTED BIBLIOGRAPHY

6. "On Virtue," pp. 224-25.
7. "Arnaut Daniel: Canzoni of his Middle Period," pp. 249-51.
8. "Canzon: Of the Trades and Love," pp. 274-75. Another Daniel translation.
9. "On Technique," pp. 297-99.
10. "On Music," pp. 343-44.
11. "En breu brisaral temps braus," pp. 369-70. A prose translation of Daniel's canzon.
12. "Three Canzoni of Arnaut Daniel," pp. 392-93.

"Prolegomena," *Poetry Review*, 1 (February 1912), 72-76. In *LE*, 8-12.

"Psychology and Troubadours," Quest, IV (October 1912), 37-53. In *SR*, 87-100.

1913

"Status Rerum," *Poetry*, 1 (January 1913), 123-27.
"A Few Don'ts by an Imagiste," *Poetry*, 1 (March 1913), 200-06. In *LE*, 4-8.
"How I Began," *T.P.'s Weekly*, xxi (June 6, 1913), 707.
"The Approach to Paris," *The New Age*, xiii (September-October 1913). Seven installments:
1. "The Approach to Paris," pp. 551-52.
2. In part, on Remy de Gourmont, pp. 577-79.
3. "Monsieur Romains, Unanimist," pp. 607-09.
4. On Charles Vildrac, pp. 631-33.
5. On Laurent Tailhade, De Regnier, and Corbiere, pp. 662-64.
6. On Francis Jammes, pp. 694-96.
7. On Rimbaud, Fort, Spire, Henri-Martin Barzun, and others, pp. 726-28.

"The Serious Artist," *The New Freewoman*, 1 (October-November 1913), 161-63, 194-95, and 213-14. In *LE*, 41-57.

235

1914

"The Tradition," *Poetry*, III (January 1914), 137-41.

"The New Sculpture," *The Egoist*, I (February 16, 1914), 67-68.

"An Essay in Constructive Criticism, with Apologies to Mr. F_D M_D_H_FF_R in the 'STOuTLOOK,' " *The Egoist*, I (February 16, 1914), 76.

"Homage to Wilfred Hunt," *Poetry*, III (March 1914), 220-23.

"The Later Yeats," *Poetry*, IV (May 1914), 64-69. In *LE*, 378-81.

"Mr. Hueffer and the Prose Tradition in Verse," *Poetry*, IV (June 1914), 111-20. In *LE*, 371-77.

"Vortex. Pound," BLAST, I (June 1914), 153-54.

" 'Dubliners' and Mr. James Joyce," *The Egoist*, I (July 15, 1914), 267.

"Vorticism," *Fortnightly Review*, XCVI (n.s.), (September 1, 1914), 461-71. In *Gaudier-Brzeska: A Memoir*, pp. 94-109.

1915

"Affirmations," *The New Age*, XVI (January-February 1915). Seven installments:

1. "Arnold Dolmetsch," pp. 246-47. In *LE*, 431-36.
2. "Vorticism," pp. 277-78.
3. "Jacob Epstein," pp. 311-12.
4. "As for Imagisme," pp. 349-50.
5. "Gaudier-Brzeska," pp. 380-82.
6. "Analysis of This Decade," pp. 409-11.
7. "The Non-Existence of Ireland," pp. 451-53.

"Webster Ford," *The Egoist*, II (January 1, 1915), 11-12.

"Imagisme and England: A Vindication and an Anthology," *T.P.'s Weekly*, XXV (February 20, 1915), 185.

236

1917

"Vers Libre and Arnold Dolmetsch," *The Egoist*, iv (July 1917), 90-91. In *LE*, 437-40.

"Elizabethan Classicists," *The Egoist*, iv and v (September 1917-January 1918), iv, 120-22, 135-36, 154-56, 168, and v, 8-9. In *LE*, 227-48.

"Irony, Lagorgue and Some Satire," *Poetry*, xi (November 1917), 93-98. In *LE*, 280-84.

1918

"A Study in French Poets," *The Little Review*, iv (February 1918), 3-61. In *Instigations*, pp. 3-105.

"The Hard and the Soft in French Poetry," *Poetry*, xi (February 1918), 264-71. In *LE*, 285-89.

"Chinese Poetry," *To-Day*, iii (April-May 1918), 54-57 and 93-95.

"Early Translations of Homer," *The Egoist*, v (August-October 1918), 95-97, 106-08, 120-21. In *LE*, 249-75.

Review of A. Waley's *170 Chinese Poems, Future*, ii. 11 (November 1918), 286-87.

1919

"The Chinese Written Character as a Medium for Poetry, by Ernest Fenollosa and Ezra Pound," *The Little Review*, vi (September-December 1919), 62-64 (September); 57-64 (October); 55-60 (November); 68-72 (December).

1920

"Arthur Symons," *The Athenaeum*, xciv (May 21, 1920), 663-64.

1939

"This Hulme Business," the *Townsman*, ii (January 1939), 15.

SELECTED BIBLIOGRAPHY

"Ford Madox (Hueffer) Ford: Obit," *The Nineteenth Century and After*, cxxvi (August 1939), 178-81.

1962

"Ezra Pound: An Interview," *The Paris Review*, 28 (Summer-Fall, 1962), 22-51.

Secondary Sources

BIBLIOGRAPHY

Donald Gallup, *A Bibliography of Ezra Pound* (London, 1965).

BIOGRAPHY

Patricia M. Hutchins, *Ezra Pound's Kensington* (London, 1965).
Eustace Mullings, *This Difficult Individual, Ezra Pound* (New York, 1961).
Charles Norman, *Ezra Pound* (New York, 1960).

REFERENCE

John H. Edwards, ed., *The Pound Newsletter*. 10 issues (Berkeley, January 1954-April 1956).
John H. Edwards and William Vasse, *Annotated Index to The Cantos of Ezra Pound* (Berkeley and Los Angeles, 1957).

CRITICISM—BOOKS

*Lawrence W. Chisholm, *Fenollosa: The Far East and American Culture* (New Haven, 1963).
Stanley Coffman, *Imagism: A Chapter in the History of Modern Poetry* (Norman, Okla., 1951).

* Items with an asterisk indicate direct or indirect criticism of *Cathay*.

*Donald Davie, *Ezra Pound: Poet as Sculptor* (New York, 1964).

George Dekker, *Sailing After Knowledge: The Cantos of Ezra Pound* (London, 1963).

L. S. Dembo, *The Confucian Odes of Ezra Pound: A Critical Appraisal* (Berkeley, 1963).

Sergei M. Eisenstein, *The Film Sense*, trans. Jay Leyda (New York, 1942).

Clark Emery, *Ideas into Action: A Study of Pound's Cantos* (Coral Gables, Fla., 1958).

John J. Espey, *Ezra Pound's Mauberley: A Study in Composition* (Berkeley and Los Angeles, 1955).

Achilles Fang, *Materials for the Studies of Pound's Cantos* (Harvard doctoral dissertation, 1958).

John Gould Fletcher, *Life Is My Song* (New York and Toronto, 1937).

G. S. Fraser, *Ezra Pound* (Edinburgh, 1960 and New York, 1961).

K. L. Goodwin, *The Influence of Ezra Pound* (London, 1966).

Glenn Hughes, *Imagism and the Imagists: A Study in Modern Poetry* (Stanford, 1931).

*Hugh Kenner, *The Poetry of Ezra Pound* (London, 1951).

Frank Kermode, *Romantic Image* (New York, 1957).

Lewis Leary, ed., *Motive and Method in The Cantos of Ezra Pound* (New York, 1954).

Guy Michaud, *Message Poétique du Symbolisme* (Paris, 1947, 3 vols.).

Earl Miner, *The Japanese Tradition in British and American Poetry* (Princeton, 1958).

N. Christoph de Nagy, *The Poetry of Ezra Pound: The Pre-Imagist Stage* (Berne, 1960).

Walter Pater, *The Renaissance* (London, 1873).

——, *Appreciations* (London, 1889).

Mario Praz, *The Romantic Agony*, 2nd edn. (Cleveland and New York, 1963).

M. L. Rosenthal, *A Primer of Ezra Pound* (New York, 1960).

Peter Russell, ed., *An Examination of Ezra Pound* (New York, 1960).

Herbert Newton Schneidau, *Ezra Pound's Criticism and the Influence of His Literary Relationships in London, 1908-1920* (Princeton dissertation, 1962).

Noel Stock, *Poet in Exile: Ezra Pound* (Manchester, 1964).

———, ed., *Ezra Pound: Perspectives* (Chicago, 1965).

———, *Reading the 'Cantos': a Study of Meaning in Ezra Pound* (London, 1967).

J. P. Sullivan, *Ezra Pound and Sextus Propertius: A Study in Creative Translation* (Austin, Texas, 1964).

Walter Sutton, ed., *Ezra Pound: A Collection of Critical Essays* (Englewood Cliffs, N.J., 1963).

Arthur Symons, *The Symbolist Movement in Literature* (London, 1899).

———, *Figures of Several Centuries* (London, 1916).

———, *Colour Studies in Paris* (London, 1918).

René Taupin, *L'Influence du symbolisme français sur la poésie américaine* (Paris, 1929).

William Van O'Connor, *Ezra Pound* (Minneapolis, 1963).

Harold H. Watts, *Ezra Pound and The Cantos* (Chicago, 1952).

Hugh Witemeyer, *Ezra Pound's Poetry 1908-1916* (Princeton dissertation, 1966).

William Butler Yeats, *Essays and Introductions* (London, 1961).

CRITICISM—ARTICLES

Richard Aldington, "Penultimate Poetry," *The Egoist*, 1 (January 15, 1914), 36.

*Richard P. Benton, "A Gloss on Pound's 'Four Poems of Departure,'" *Literature East and West*, x.3 (September 1906), 292-301.

R. P. Blackmur, "The Masks of Ezra Pound," and "An Adjunct to the Muses' Diadem" in *Form and Value in Modern Poetry* (New York, 1957).

Thomas E. Connolly, "Ezra Pound's 'Near Perigord' The Background of a Poem," *Comparative Literature*, VIII (1956), 110-21.

T. S. Eliot, *"Ezra Pound: His Metric and Poetry" (1917) in *To Criticize the Critic* (New York, 1965).

————, "The Method of Mr. Pound" *The Athenaeum* (October 24, 1919), 1065-66.

————, "Introduction" to *Selected Poems of Ezra Pound* (London, 1928).

————, "The Noh and the Image" *The Egoist*, IV.7 (August 1917), 102ff.

Achilles Fang, "A Note on Pound's 'Papyrus,'" *Modern Languages Notes*, LXVII (1952), 188-90.

————, *"Fenollosa and Pound," *Harvard Journal of Asian Studies*, XX (1957), 213-38.

*John Gould Fletcher, "The Orient and Contemporary Poetry," in *The Asian Legacy and American Life*, ed. A. Christy (New York, 1945), pp. 145-74.

F. S. Flint, "Imagisme," *Poetry*, I (January 1913), 198-200.

————, "A History of Imagism," *The Egoist*, II (May 1, 1915), 70-71.

*A. C. Graham, Introduction to *Poems of the Late T'ang* (Baltimore, 1965).

*Hsieh, Wen Tung, "English Translations of Chinese Poetry," *Criterion*, LXVIII (April 1938), 402-24.

T. E. Hulme, "A Lecture on Modern Poetry" in *Further Speculations*, ed. Sam Hynes (Minneapolis, 1955).

A. R. Jones, "The Poetic Theory," Chapter III of *The Life and Opinions of Thomas Ernest Hulme* (Boston, 1960).

241

A. R. Jones, "Notes Toward a History of Imagism," *South Atlantic Quarterly*, LX (Summer 1961), 262-85.

*George Kennedy, "Fenollosa, Pound and the Chinese Character," *Yale Literary Magazine*, CXXVI (December 1958), 24-26.

Hugh Kenner, *Introduction to *The Translations of Ezra Pound* (New Directions, 1953).

———, "The Broken Mirrors and the Mirror of Memory," in *Motive and Method in The Cantos of Ezra Pound*, ed. Lewis Leary (New York, 1954).

———, *"Ezra Pound and Chinese," *Agenda*, IV (October-November 1965), 38-41.

———, *"The Invention of China," *Spectrum*, IX.1 (Spring 1967), 21-52.

F. R. Leavis, Chapter on Pound in *New Bearings in English Poetry* (London, 1932).

*William McNaughton, "Ezra Pound et la littérature chinoise," *Ezra Pound* (Paris, 1965), II, 508-17.

*Earl Miner, "Pound, Haiku, and the Image," *Hudson Review*, IX (Winter 1956-57), 570-84.

*Pen-ti Lee and Donald Murray, "The Quality of *Cathay*: Ezra Pound's Early Translations of Chinese Poems," *Literature East and West*, x.3 (September 1966), 264-77.

*Angela Jung Palendri, " 'The Stone Is Alive in My Hand'— Ezra Pound's Chinese Translations," *Literature East and West*, x.3 (September 1966), 278-91.

Walter Pater, "The School of Giorgione," *Renaissance*, pp. 134, 149-50. "Coleridge," *Appreciations*, pp. 66-68.

R. H. Pearce, "Toward an American Epic," *The Hudson Review* (Autumn 1959).

*Hugh Gordon Porteus, "Ezra Pound and His Chinese Characters: A Radical Examination" in Peter Russell, ed., *Ezra Pound: A Collection of Essays* (London, 1950), pp. 203-17.

Edgar Allan Poe, "The Philosophy of Composition," *Works*, XIV, 195.

Sister Bernetta Quinn, "The Metamorphoses of Ezra Pound," in *Motive and Method in The Cantos of Ezra Pound*, ed. Lewis Leary (New York, 1954). Reprinted in Quinn, *The Metaphoric Tradition in Modern Poetry* (New Brunswick, N.J., 1955).

Herbert Schneidau, "Pound and Yeats: The Question of Symbolism," *ELH*, xxxii (1965), 220-37.

Kenneth Sisam, Letter on Pound's *Seafarer*, *TLS* (June 25, 1954).

Edith Sitwell, "Ezra Pound" in Russell, ed., *An Examination of Ezra Pound* (New York, 1950).

Lytton Strachey, "An Anthology" (1908) in *Characters and Commentaries* (New York, 1933), pp. 140-41.

Arthur Symons, "The Decadent Movement in Literature," *Harper's* (November 1893), pp. 859ff.

*Arthur Waley, *The Poet Li Po, A.D. 701-762* (London, 1918).

C. B. Willard, "Ezra Pound's Debt to Walt Whitman," *Studies in Philology*, liv (1957), 573-81.

William Carlos Williams, Introduction to *Kora in Hell: Improvisations* (Boston, 1920).

On Translation

Reuben Arthur Brower, ed., *On Translation* (Cambridge, Mass., 1959). Contains comprehensive bibliography from 46 B.C. to 1958 compiled by Bayard Quincy Morgan.

William Arrowsmith and Roger Shattuck, eds., *The Craft and Context of Translation: A Critical Symposium* (Austin, Texas, 1961). Contains brilliant essays on the new conventions in translations.

Since Brower's book contains excellent brief summaries of the items listed in the bibliography, I need not repeat them here but simply list those related to the present discussion:

Achilles Fang, "Some Reflections on the Difficulty of Translation," in Brower, pp. 111-33.

Jean Paris, "Translation and Creation," in Arrowsmith and Shattuck, pp. 57-67.

Roy Earl Teele, *Through a Glass Darkly: A Study of English Translations of Chinese Poetry* (Ann Arbor, 1949).

I. A. Richards, *Mencius on the Mind: Experiments in Multiple Definitions* (London, 1932).

Introduction to *Ying-hua-chi*, a comparative collection of English translations of Chinese poetry (reprinted in Taipei, Taiwan, 1959)—text in Chinese.

Wang Li, *Han-yü Shih-lü-hsüeh* (*The Prosody of Chinese Poetry*), (Shanghai, 1962)—text in Chinese.

James J. Y. Liu, *The Art of Chinese Poetry* (Chicago, 1962). So far the only book in English to deal intelligently with the art of Chinese poetry.

See also the introduction to individual works of translation of Chinese poetry listed in the next section; see especially Hervey-Saint-Denys, Waley, Hawkes, and A. C. Graham.

English Translations of Chinese Poetry
(*In chronological order*)

1761   [Bishop Thomas Percy], *Hau Kiou Choaan* or *The Pleasing History* (London, 4 vols., 1761).

1809   Stephen Weston, *Le Tang, An Imperial Poem in Chinese by Kien Lung* (London, 1809).

(1867)   Judith Gautier, *Le Livre de Jade* (Paris, 1867).

1870   John Francis Davis, *Poeseos Sinicae Commentarii* (London, 1870).

(1872)   Marie J. L. Marquis d' Hervey de Saint-Denys, *Poésies de l'époque des Thang* (Paris, 1872).

1871   James Legge, *The She King* in *The Chinese Classics* IV (London, 1871).

1876   James Legge, *The She King*, or *The Book of Ancient Poetry, Translated in English Verse* (London, 1876).

1884   H. A. Giles, *Gems of Chinese Literature* (Shanghai, 1884).

1890   Stuart Merrill, *Pastels in Prose* (New York, 1890). Translations from *Le Livre de Jade*.

1891   C.R.F. Allen, *Book of Chinese Poetry* (London, 1891).

1891   William Jennings, *The Shi King*, the Old "Poetry Classic" of the Chinese, A Close Metrical Translation with Annotations (London, 1891).

1901   H. A. Giles, *History of Chinese Literature* (New York, 1901).

1901   W.A.P. Martin, *Lore of Cathay* (Edinburgh and London, 1901).

1902   L. Cranmer-Byng, *The Never Ending Wrong and Other Renderings* (London, 1902).

1907   J. Dyer Ball, *Rhythms and Rhymes in Chinese Climes* (Hong Kong, 1907).

1909   L. Cranmer-Byng, *A Lute of Jade*, Wisdom of the East Series (London, 1909).

1910   Clifford Bax, *Twenty Chinese Poems* (Hempstead, 1910).

1912   Charles Budd, *Chinese Poems* (London, 1912).

1912   W.A.P. Martin, *Chinese Legends and Lyrics* (Shanghai, 1912).

1913   Helen Waddel, *Lyrics from the Chinese* (London, 1913).

1915   Ezra Pound, *Cathay* (London, 1915).

1916   Clifford Bax, *Twenty-Five Chinese Poems* (London, 1916).

1916   L. Cranmer-Byng, *A Feast of Lanterns*. Wisdom of the East Series (London, 1916).

1916   Arthur Waley, *Chinese Poems* (London, 1916). (Reprint 1965.)

1918   James Whitall, *Chinese Lyrics* (translations from *Le Livre de Jade*), (New York, 1918).

1919   Arthur Waley, *A Hundred and Seventy Chinese Poems* (New York, 1919).

1919   W.J.B. Fletcher, *Gems of Chinese Poetry* (Shanghai, 1919).

1919   T. Gaunt, *A Little Garland from Cathay* (Shanghai, 1919).

1920   L. Cranmer-Byng, *The Book of Odes* (Shi King). Wisdom of the East Series (London, 1920).

1921   Florence Ayscough and Amy Lowell, *Fir-Flower Tablets* (New York, 1921).

1922   Shigeyosha Obata, *The Works of Li Po* (New York, 1922).

1923   Arthur Waley, *The Temple* (New York, 1923).

1927   Ian Calvin, *After the Chinese* (London, 1927).

1929   Florence Ayscough, *Tu Fu, The Autobiography of a Chinese Poet* (London, 1929).

1929   Witter Bynner, *The Jade Mountain* (New York, 1929).

1929   Arthur Christy, *Images in Jade* (New York, 1929).

1929   Lim Boon Keng, *The Li Sao, An Elegy on Encountering Sorrows* (Shanghai, 1929).

1929   V.W.W.S. Purcell, *The Spirit of Chinese Poetry* (Shanghai, 1929).

1929   Edna Worthley Underwood, *Tu Fu, Wanderer and Minstrel under Moons of Cathay* (Portland, Maine, 1929).

1931   Henry H. Hart, *A Chinese Market* (Peking, 1931).

1932   Marcel Granet, *Festivals and Songs in Ancient China*. Trans. E. D. Edwards (London, 1932).

1932   Ts'ai Ting-kan, *Chinese Poems in English Rhymes* (Chicago, 1932).

1933   W.J.B. Fletcher, *More Gems of Chinese Poetry* (Shanghai, 1933).

1933   Clara Caudlin, *The Herald Wind*, translations of Sung Dynasty poems. Wisdom of the East Series (London, 1933).

1934   Florence Ayscough, *Travels of a Chinese Poet, Tu Fu, Guest of Rivers and Lakes* (London, 1934).

1934   A. J. Brace, *Tu Fu, China's Great Poet* (poems written in Szechwan) (Ch'engtu, China, 1934).

(1935)   Sung-nien Hsu, *Li Thai-po* (Lyon, 1935).

1935   Cyril Drummond Le Gros Clark, *The Prose-Poetry of Su Tung-p'o* (Shanghai, 1935).

1936   Harold Acton and Ch'en Shih-hsiang, *Modern Chinese Poetry* (London, 1936).

1937   Ch'u Ta-kao, *Chinese Lyrics* (Cambridge, 1937).

1938   Henry H. Hart, *A Garden of Peonies* (Stanford, 1938).

1938   Evangelin D. Edwards, *The Dragon Book* (London, 1938).

1938   Henry Hart, *The Hundred Names* (Berkeley, 1938).

1939   Jen Tai, *Everlasting Woe* (Shanghai, 1938).

1940   Soame Jenyns, *Selections from the Three Hundred Poems of the T'ang Dynasty*. Wisdom of the East Series (London, 1920).

1944   Soame Jenyns, *A Further Selection from the Three Hundred Poems of the T'ang Dynasty*. Wisdom of the East Series (London, 1944).

1946   Gerald Bullett, *The Golden Year of Fan Ch'eng-ta* (Cambridge, 1946).

1946   Clara Caudlin, *The Rapier of Lu*. Wisdom of the East Series (London, 1946).

1946   Powys Mathews, *Love Songs of Asia* (New York, 1946).

1947   Lin Yu-t'ang, *The Gay Genius* (New York, 1947).

1947   Robert Payne, *Contemporary Chinese Poetry* (London, 1947).

1947   Robert Payne, *The White Pony* (New York, 1947).

1948   Arthur Waley, *Chinese Poems* (London, 1948).

1949   Arthur Waley, *The Life and Times of Po Chü-i* (London, 1949).

1950   Bernhard Karlgren, *The Book of Odes* (Stockholm, 1950).

1950   Arthur Waley, *The Poetry and Career of Li Po* (New York, 1950).

1952   William Acker, *T'ao the Hermit* (New York, 1952).

1952   William Hung, *Tu Fu: China's Greatest Poet* (Cambridge, Mass., 1952).

1953   Yang Hsien-yi and Gladys Yang, *The Li Sao and Other Poems of Ch'ü Yüan* (Peking, 1953).

195?   Wong Man, *Poems from China* (Hong Kong, n.d.).

1954   Ezra Pound, *The Classical Anthology Defined by Confucius* (Cambridge, Mass., 1954).

1958   Gary Synder, *Riprap & Cold Mountain Poems* (San Francisco, 1965). (Reprint from *Evergreen Review*, 1958.)

1958   C. H. Kwock and Vincent McHugh, *Why I Live on the Mountain* (San Francisco, 1958).

(1958)   E. Von Zach, *Die Chinesische Anthologie* (Cambridge, Mass., 1958).

1959   David Hawkes, *Ch'u Tz'u: The Songs of the South* (Oxford, 1959).

1960   C. J. Chen and Michael Bullock, *Poems of Solitude* (London, 1960).

1960   Arthur Waley, *Ballads and Stories from Tun-huang* (London, 1960).

1962   James J. Y. Liu, *The Art of Chinese Poetry* (Chicago, 1962).

1962   A. R. Davis, ed., *The Penguin Book of Chinese Verse* (London, 1962).

(1962)   Paul Demieville, *Anthologie de la Poésie Chinoise Classique* (Paris, 1962).

1962   Burton Watson, *Early Chinese Literature* (New York, 1962).

1963   Hsu Kai-yu, *Twentieth Century Chinese Poetry: An Anthology* (New York, 1963).

1965   Burton Watson, *Su Tung-p'o* (New York, 1965).

1965   A. C. Graham, *Poems of the Late T'ang* (Baltimore, 1965).

1965   Alan Ayling and Duncan Mackintosh, *A Collection of Chinese Lyrics* (London, 1965).

1965   Cyril Birch, ed., *Anthology of Chinese Literature* (New York, 1965).

1967   David Hawkes, *A Little Primer of Tu Fu* (Oxford, 1967).

1967   J. D. Frodsham and Ch'eng Hsi, *An Anthology of Chinese Verse* (Oxford, 1967).

indexes

Index to Names

Index to Titles by Pound

253

INDEX

254

Index to Titles by Others

Index to Important Concepts, Topics, and Terms

258